REAL-WORLD
NONDUALITY
–Reports from the Field

NSP

NEW SARUM PRESS

UNITED KINGDOM

New Sarum Press, 6 Folkestone Road, Salisbury, SP2 8JP, U.K.
www.newsarumpress.com
First printing December 2018
ISBN: 978-1-9993535-1-3
Cover image: *My Child Is My World* by Robert Saltzman

Real-World Nonduality
—Reports from the Field

Table of Contents

Introduction by Greg Goode vii

Synopses xiii

Acknowledgements xix

The Direct Path and Parenting *by Kavitha Chinnaiyan* 1

Religion and the Direct Path *by Terry Moore* 15

Confessions of an Experience Junkie *by Steve Diamond* 28

The Windows in My Head *by Zachary Rodecap* 43

The Direct Path and Causality *by Priscilla Francis* 55

Release the Releaser *by James N. Hurley* 71

An Enquiry into Space *by Kim Lai* 85

When Two and Two Are Really One *by David Boulter* 96

The Direct Path and Emptiness *by Sandra Pippa* 110

Berkeley and Blake: An Extended Look at Objectivity
by John Lamont-Black 124

Any Day Now I Shall Be Released: On Not Being
"Finished" on the Direct Path *by Stephen Joseph* 144

About the Authors... 155

Reading List... 160

Appendix: The Heart Opener 163

Index... 165

Introduction
by Greg Goode

Many years ago I attended a week-long retreat given by a well-known teacher of nonduality. There was a group of psychotherapists present, and this was their first exposure to the message of nonduality. I happened to be sitting near them during the morning break. They were excited but confused, and I heard a bit of their discussion.

"This changes everything."

"We must completely rethink psychotherapy."

"Let's have an emergency meeting after lunch."

This happened almost two decades ago, before the advent of the specialty sometimes called "nondual psychotherapy." It's just one example of what happens when everyday life encounters nonduality.

This is a book of essays by new writers about how their encounters with nonduality have impacted their lives (see *Note from 2018*, page x). I'll say more about nonduality below, but briefly, I mean the intimacy and inseparability of things. For many people, as well as those psychotherapists, the first encounter with nonduality can feel shocking.

What about the other areas of life? Those areas are what this book is about. The essays here discuss what happens to a wide variety of life situations when nonduality enters the picture: career, parenting, traditional religion, addiction, disease, death, perception, thought, and the very idea of being "enlightened."

The Direct Path Approach to Nonduality

There are many possible approaches to nonduality. The approach referred to in these essays is the "direct path" teaching that flows from Sri Atmananda (Krishna Menon) and those who have been influenced by his work, including Jean Klein, John Levy, Ananda Wood, Francis Lucille, Rupert Spira, myself, and a few others. I've included a short reading list at the end of this collection (p.160).

We will be discussing how this approach and the insights that come with it may be woven into daily life. It is deeply experiential, not theoretical. It begins with the intuition of a sweet, abiding clarity that seems to lie behind experiences and seems to illuminate at least the pleasant ones. We bring our attention to this clarity in various ways, such as self-inquiry, body-sensing yoga, resting as awareness, mini-reminders, guided meditation, and even long walks. We discover that clarity and sweetness illuminate all experiences. This is because clarity is the nature of experience. And sweetness is the aroma of clarity.

I'm sure that essays like the ones in this book could be written about many other varieties of nondual teaching as well. The direct path is just one way to talk about nonduality. It is not new or unique.

Regular people tell it like it is

But this book does offer something new. It offers a series of views from the trenches. The writers are new at writing about nonduality. They are not claiming enlightenment. They are not writing from the perspective of a guru or satsang teacher. They are regular people writing in a down-to-earth way about how nonduality has impacted their lives. They are discussing situations faced by students of nonduality everywere.

This approach is different. It may even be revolutionary.

Many texts on this subject are written in a "mountaintop" style, as though the author has ascended to some important level, proclaiming down to the reader. If Martians were to land on earth and examine the average nonduality library, they'd conclude that this is the only way to communicate.

Several of our writers have noticed this too. In discussing their backgrounds with me, they mentioned being told by teachers that, "only the enlightened should write about spiritual topics." The argument goes that if anyone else tried, they'd cause "a loss of purity." This would result in "the blind leading the blind."

We are ignoring these directives, for several good reasons. First, what is being said when a teacher utters these things?

"I am enlightened and pure; I can write about these things. You aren't, so you can't."

Besides sounding arrogant and narcissistic, this pronouncement takes itself seriously. It assumes a world view that nondual inquiry subjects to deep scrutiny. Nonduality examines the idea of an enlightened or unenlightened person and finds the idea to be nonsense. This is primarily because the more we search for "who" is enlightened or unenlightened, the less we find. And secondarily, most nonduality teachings caution us against taking seriously the adjectives "enlightened" and "unenlightened." These labels are like any others, such as "teacher," "student," or "construction worker." Even if they function in practical, day-to-day matters, they fail to refer to anything findable, anything really present.

We are ignoring these anti-writing directives mainly because there's no way to put communication in a box. No one can control it. Spiritual writing is already too vast. Writing to teach, to "lead," is just one mode. We have teacherly tomes in nonduality, some of which I have written. We have masterful collections of dialogues with Ramana Maharshi, Nisargadatta Maharaj, and Sri Atmananda (Krishna Menon).

But communication doesn't have to be didactic. For example, Buddhism has generated many modes of spiritual writing. But as far as I know, nonduality has nothing that parallels works like Rodger Kamenetz's well-known *The Jew in the Lotus*,[1] Georges Dreyfus's insightful *The Sound of Two Hands Clapping*,[2] or David Chadwick's fascinating *Thank You and OK!: An American Zen Failure in Japan*.[3]

I simply can't find any reason that reportorial, confessional, and observant pieces like these shouldn't exist in the field of nonduality. Perhaps this book is a small start. Readers may find it a useful springboard to look at nonduality from different angles or learn that someone else is experiencing the same issues they are going through.

In the next section you will find synopses of the essays that follow. I've chosen a rough order that proceeds from more concrete issues to more abstract ones.

Note from 2018

Writing in November 2018, I look back and see that this book has been in the works for more than three years. It's been a coordinated effort among writers, editors and proofreaders. Because the group consisted of new, unpublished writers, we even enlisted the services of a professional writing coach (along with yours truly) to help those who requested it. In the early days, we even had exercises and practice assignments!

---

1.   Kamenetz, R. (2009) *The Jew in the Lotus: A Poet's Rediscovery of Jewish Identity in Buddhist India*, Harper One
2.   Dreyfus, G. (2003) *The Sound of Two Hands Clapping: The Education of a Tibetan Buddhist Monk*, University of California Press
3.   Chadwick, D. (2007) *Thank You and OK!: An American Zen Failure in Japan*, Shambhala

Since the project began in July, 2015, we've had life changes, illnesses, recuperations, and death in the family. People have moved house, changed their day jobs, retired, taken up hobbies and passionate new interests in life. And some people have begun writing, publishing and conducting spiritual teaching. I mention this because when the project began all our contributors were indeed new writers. But by the time this book became available, several have been writing and sharing elsewhere.

Note on UK English and US English Spelling

Individual essays may have USA or UK English spelling, as appropriate to each author's background.

About the proceeds

We will be donating the proceeds from this book to the Centre Against Abuse in Bermuda (www.centreagainstabuse.bm).

Synopses

PARENTING

Kavitha Chinnaiyan writes about her two daughters and the impact nonduality has had on her parenting. She discusses how various kinds of meditations have helped her avoid projecting her own hopes, desires, and identity issues upon her two daughters. These meditations have helped Kavitha see her daughters for what they are, and not as miniature versions of herself. Nonduality has helped her love in a more unconditional way.

RELIGION

Terry Moore has been a member of a Sufi order for many years. He writes about encountering nonduality after practicing Sufism for a long time. Sufism, as he was practicing it, had become dry and conceptual. Nonduality and its inquiries into experience helped Terry discover the experiential elements already present in Sufism, along with their concomitant liveliness and joy.

ADDICTION TO PEAK STATES

In "Confessions of an Experience Junkie," Steve Diamond describes his former addiction to subtle spiritual states, and how the addiction dissipated with the help of nondual inquiry. Steve was caught in a tricky cycle with those states, which would never remain permanently. Not only did he seek these states for the good feelings that resulted, but he also interpreted them as signs of enlightenment. Through nondual inquiry, however, Steve realized that what he really wanted from these states was always present as his true nature.

PERCEPTION

Zachary Rodecap discusses how his materialist worldview was severely challenged by nonduality. He was accustomed to thinking of his senses and mind as providing an accurate picture of how the world is. But this way of thinking is subjected to radical investigation in nonduality. Zachary discusses his struggles with this investigation, as well as a key insight that helped him along the way.

CAUSALITY

Priscilla Francis writes about causality. As an inquisitive child, she enjoyed investigating life. But as she matured and encountered disconcerting life situations, her investigations turned solemn and distressing. At this point Priscilla longed to be rid of her tormenting doubts on the substance and significance of life. Her fervor inspired her to explore a wide range of spiritual options. When she discovered nonduality, she found that the nondual approach to causality helped her see her compelling questions in a very different light. As she found freedom from her need for absolute answers, she discovered that many aspects of day-to-day living became lighter and freer as well.

SPIRITUAL IDENTITY

James Hurley discusses how nonduality helped him get past a roadblock put up by another path. As a practitioner and teacher of the Sedona Method, James was able to release any unpleasant feelings that came up, but he still hadn't found the lasting peace he was looking for. Through guidance from a nonduality teacher, James realized how the Sedona Method was a valuable technique for working with feelings, but not the tool to go "all the way." At some point, even the Method must be released, as well as the "releaser" identity it can create.

SPACE

Kim Lai writes about his difficulties inquiring into the notion of "space." Kim had always liked spacious places like ocean horizons and mountaintops, and had taken space and physical objects for granted as foundational parts of reality. But he didn't think about space as a concept until he became interested in nonduality. Kim heard a lot of nonduality teachers dismiss space as illusory. But since space seemed so real to him, he concluded that he'd better do some inquiry about it. He recounts some of his contemplations and shows how spatial assumptions pervade our thinking. These assumptions can even work their way into nondual inquiry. But spatial assumptions are not necessary, and Kim describes how he was finally able to realize the nondual nature of space.

TRUTH

David Boulter, a mathematics teacher, discusses how nondual inquiry helped free him from the need to have true conceptual answers to his metaphysical questions. He recounts an inquiry about mathematical truth. What about the supposedly rock-solid truth "2+2=4"? We think of it as reliable a truth as anything can be, and counting on such truths can be comforting. But nonduality would consider it a mere concept with no reference to anything objectively true. In view of nonduality, David considers the question, is math just false? Does nondual insight mean that he should quit his job and go join an ashram?

EMPTINESS

Sandra Pippa recounts how studying Madhyamaka Buddhism[4] made a significant impact on the way she engages with nonduality. Years ago, when she first met with nonduality in the School of Practical Philosophy, she found it to be a deeply inspiring message wrapped up in a dogmatic and sexist social context. By studying the Madhyamaka emptiness approach, Sandra was able to gain freedom from the type of thinking that attributes objective truth to spiritual teachings. This freedom allowed her to distinguish the timeless spiritual message of nonduality from certain socially flawed presentations, and gave her a more liberated appreciation of the direct path.

EXISTENCE

John Lamont-Black writes as a scientist who struggled with objectivity, the idea that things exist outside of awareness. Objectivity felt convincing and obvious to him. But in nonduality, this feeling is held to be the root of our sense of separation and angst. John describes an attempt he made to explain objectivity, so that objectivity would be compatible with nondualism. But in deeper inquiry, he discovered his explanation, and conception of objectivity itself, to be nothing more than mythical.

ENLIGHTENMENT

In the touching essay "Any Day Now I Shall Be Released," Stephen Joseph describes the frustration of fifteen years on the

---

4. Madhyamaka states that all phenomena are empty, so that they have no independent essence or solid, separate existence. All phenomena arise only in relation to other phenomena and thus everything is mutually dependent on everything else for its existence.

nondual path without a successful conclusion. This has meant fifteen years of wanting "enlightenment" but not achieving it. Stephen discusses the self-doubts and feelings of inadequacy that can accompany nondual inquiry. And even though these very feelings can be subjected to nondual inquiry, his desire for the goal remains. His frustration has made him wonder whether there are more suitable paths for him. But so far, the most promising approach has been to investigate the various assumptions behind the idea of "being done."

****

The essays in this book illustrate the many ways that non-duality affects daily life. The writers come from many different countries. Since nonduality is about everything, nothing is left out. So it's natural that people will have struggles as well as triumphs. Nonduality is also a culturally "thin" teaching. Besides encouraging insight and love, it doesn't prescribe what we should think or do in life. This openness leaves room for nondual wisdom to manifest itself in many ways.

Acknowledgments

I'd like to thank the Radius Foundation, whose kind support made possible the editorial services of Abigail Tardiff. This book features essays from new writers, most of whom have never written at length about the topics herein. Consequently, Abby's sharp eye, encouraging presence, and love for the written word have been immensely helpful.

The Direct Path and Parenting
by Kavitha Chinnaiyan

" My children are my greatest teachers. They hold up for my inspection all the beliefs and views that remain from my long-standing conditioning. The process of raising them brings up my greatest fears, limitations, and flaws. They give me no room for inauthenticity and demand total honesty in all my dealings, even those that don't involve them. They call me out on disparities, bringing my hidden inner conflicts to the surface. Their innocent eyes illuminate the dark places in me where fears and anxieties form the unseen strings that manipulate their lives. "

Like most parents, I can divide my life neatly into two parts: the one before my children came along and the one after. When I held my newborn for the first time, I felt my heart fall away into a space I had not known existed. I tried speaking to this beautiful creature, finding that no word seemed adequate in that glimpse into absolute love. When her sister arrived two years later, I hadn't anticipated that this sense of falling away would deepen as it did. I stroked her head with its mass of curls, once again unable to speak for fear of breaking the spell. The sweetness that each of them brought to my world was akin to mystical experiences of my own distant childhood. I've grown and evolved along with my children.

I was called to the spiritual path when my daughters were toddlers. This calling was so acute and powerful that despite the constraints of juggling my demanding full-time job and raising young children, I was impelled to make time for spiritual practices. I would wake up at four in the morning to meditate before they stirred. At night, I meditated in their room while they fell asleep. For several years, my life revolved around practices, kids, and work.

1

The Direct Path

When I came to the direct path, I had been meditating regularly for a few years in the Advanced Yoga Practices (AYP) tradition. My introduction to the direct path was through Greg Goode's *Standing as Awareness*.[5] Halfway through the book, a profound shift had occurred. Instead of seeing myself as a body-mind to whom awareness arose, I knew I was awareness to whom the body-mind appeared. There was a dropping away of suffering related to wrong identification or taking myself to be the body-mind. With the dropping away of suffering, life has become simpler.

The beauty of this path is the freedom it grants us to be engaged in life while continuing the inquiry. We need not give up our jobs and relationships in order to make spiritual progress. We don't *have* to go away to an exotic ashram or change our lifestyles. Spiritual growth and blossoming can occur through ordinary life and experiences, even while we fulfill our duties to family and society.

The prerequisite for the direct path is "higher reasoning," as Sri Atmananda Krishna Menon calls it. Higher reasoning is the intuitive ability to differentiate between subject and object, as inquiry proceeds systematically from gross physical objects to the subtle objects of the mind. With "ripening," the subtle separation between the subject and the object eventually collapses into *nondual* realization. When we stand as awareness, the result of inquiry is the clarity of knowledge combined with the sweetness of love. In parenting, this clear love takes on a new dimension in our interactions with our children, even when they are challenging or unpleasant.

Since parenting is rich with experiences and elicits many emotions, thoughts, and beliefs, it provides continuous fodder for inquiry. In the way we parent our children and behave with

5.   See Reading List p.160

them, we come face-to-face with the gross and subtle structures that keep us separate and ego-bound. In day-to-day living as a householder with a busy career and countless details to attend to, the direct path is a powerful tool for transcending inner conflict and discovering the joy of being. Additionally, the responses that our children evoke in us act as true tests of our progress along the path.

Inquiry acts as a spade to unearth the many inconsistencies in the subtle and confusing messages that we pass on to our children. For example, we might tell our children that happiness does not depend upon achievements. And yet, our parenting style might include a strong emphasis on getting ahead or on distant goals of higher education, fame, and wealth—the very things we eschew externally.

The direct path opens us to seeing our children for who they really are. We come to see that they have never been ours to own. They may have our noses and our skin tones, but they are unique strands in the vast fabric of the universe, without which its grandeur is unimaginable. Our kids aren't smaller versions of ourselves, waiting to be molded into our own likeness. Yet, this attempt to force our children into our own image can be the default mode of operation in parenting. We may be so entrenched in our own views, problems, agendas, interests, and ambitions that we do not pause to think whether this molding is conducive to the way these unique strands fit into the fabric of the universe.

My children are my greatest teachers. They hold up for my inspection all the beliefs and views that remain from my long-standing conditioning. The process of raising them brings up my greatest fears, limitations, and flaws. They give me no room for inauthenticity and demand total honesty in all my dealings, even those that don't involve them. They call me out on disparities, bringing my hidden inner conflicts to the surface. Their innocent eyes illuminate the dark places in me where fears and anxieties form the unseen strings that manipulate their lives. In this new light, I find that my goals for them have more to do with me. In every interaction with them, I am given the choice between continuing along the horizontal[6] paradigm of time and space made up of instructions, chiding, rewards, goals, and consequences, or relaxing into the vertical paradigm of surrendering to the mystery of the Now.

The ego in parenting

False identification is the basis of all the suffering we create for ourselves and others. In this "normal" mode of functioning, we take ourselves to be either the body or the mind, or a combination of the two. When we identify as a body-mind in early childhood, we form an image in our heads of the "I." This "I" is built on approval and attention from our parents, teachers, and peers and from ourselves. We then proceed to live our lives conforming to this image. We struggle to control our circumstances, our family, and our friends and colleagues to keep the precious image of the "I" intact.

Some time ago, I was doing teaching rounds in the hospital where I work and was asked to consult on a pregnant woman with a serious inherited vascular condition. She was a highly educated and well-informed nurse and knew that her child had a 50% chance of inheriting the genetic defect. I heard judgmental whispers among the trainees: "How could she think of having a child, knowing the risk?" Finishing rounds, I corralled the team into a conference room. One of the trainees was pregnant and most of the others had children. I asked them, "Why did you all decide to have kids?" They took turns answering: "I wanted to experience motherhood"; "I felt it was time for me to

---

6. *Living is to be found in the timeless Now* by Jean Klein (https://not-two.net/teachers-and-sages/jean-klein/. Accessed 13 Aug, 2018). See also Reading List p.160

go to the next phase of life"; "I wanted to feel fulfilled"; and so on. I smilingly pointed out that their intentions to have children did not differ from that of the patient we had just seen—having children to actualize *their* own needs. It was no different for me.

When I began to think about having children, I thought it would be fulfilling, enriching, beautiful, and challenging—for me. Only in passing did I think about the future children's wishes, idiosyncrasies, and personalities. I simply assumed that these children would be new and improved versions of their parents—smart, self-driven, talented, and basically flawless. Little did I know that these little beings would take every opportunity to smash my carefully constructed "I" with their stubbornness, independence, and personalities that did not match my expectations!

The first false assumption in parenting is that we own our children. This assumption leads to several other beliefs, actions, and consequences. For instance, we use our children in subtle ways to enhance our self-image, the "I." We dump our unlived dreams and unrealized fantasies onto them, feeding them an image of who they *should* be. We place upon their fragile shoulders the heavy mantle of responsibility for making us happy, sad, proud, disappointed, and so on. In this displacement of responsibility, we unwittingly contribute to the creation of their own self-image or the "I" that they will struggle to conform to for the rest of their lives. Even though we love our children deeply and as unconditionally as is humanly possible, our subtle intentions to enhance our self-image through them can be hidden under false projections of altruism. We create suffering for our children and for ourselves when we believe that our behaviors serve to further their best interest.

Our children are our mirrors

My friend Shanti asked me for advice about her five-year-old daughter, who was affectionate and giving by nature. She loved to make homemade gifts for her friends and was hurt easily when they did not reciprocate in kind. When she broke down in tears and tantrums, Shanti was quick to promise her gifts and treats to get her to stop crying. I asked Shanti if she believed that her child's friends should reciprocate with gifts and attention. She hesitantly replied in the affirmative. It hurt her to see her child's efforts being dismissed; in her helplessness, she tried to make up for this lack by buying her things.

Most often, circumstances like these point to our own minds and actions. We pass on our beliefs to our children in subtle, non-verbal ways; hence the saying that they are much more likely to do what we do rather than what we say. Our beliefs and stances are plainly evident in the tone of our voices, our criticism of others (or ourselves), our behavior with people in front of and behind their backs, our response to the world's (and our own) shortcomings, what we really value, and so on. Our children mirror our behaviors perfectly.

Thus, if my child has the belief that giving must result in a similar gesture from her friends, I need to look at how I might be contributing as a model for this behavior. Do I give with reservations and expectations, or do I give freely of myself as an expression of joy and love? For example, do I really give unreservedly to my spouse? If my concept of a strong intimate relationship is one of giving to get something in return, I can never teach my children to give unreservedly. The barter model of give-and-take is more about taking than about giving, in which we covertly manipulate the other person to get things our way. This behavior does not end at home. It permeates all our interactions. At work and in the community, we give only when there is something in it for me. If there is no promise of personal gain, we are less likely to be interested in giving. Even service-oriented activities are performed to collect credit or to earn praise, or as material for college applications. Our children pick up these mind games and begin to own them, integrating them into their sense of self, their "I." We cannot expect our children to rise above their "I" if we haven't done so ourselves.

The "I" is the ego and is fragile by nature; it employs every tactic in the book to feel more secure and complete. For the ego, giving is a disaster because it feels threatened by someone else having more. The inherent insecurity of the ego is also the driving force for pushing our children to succeed. When my children succeed, I feel good and validated for having done my job so well. When they fail, I feel like a failure and it hurts.

When we want our children to earn praise for being talented, smart, capable, strong, and so on, we would benefit by questioning our motives. When we encourage lack of transparency in order to come out on top, we place winning at all costs higher than joy and freedom. When we push our children to be recognized every single time they venture out, we plant the seeds of insecurity and fear of failure. We can never teach our children graciousness, equanimity, and the path to inner freedom if we are caught up in the drama of the ego.

What is the greatest gift I can give my children? This question is worth its weight in gold for parents. From the contrasting experiences of suffering and freedom in my own life, I know what I wish for them: to discover that who they are is beyond definition, and beyond wanting, grasping for, or needing completion. They are already complete, perfect, and full.

The process of inquiry

My husband and I grew up valuing academic achievement. One of our daughters is feisty, bubbly, and stubborn, while the other is studious, mellow, and easy-going. In early elementary school, we began to notice how they differed in their attitude towards school work. While the older, studious child made getting straight A's look easy, the younger one showed little interest in grades or school work. For the better part of a year, we were on her case.

While we did everything to "help" her, she merely ignored us, refusing to let our anxieties change her performance in school.

One day, she came back home with a C. Instead of lecturing her, I was drawn to sit with my disappointment. Holding off on reacting, I took several days to inquire deeply into this anxiety. I proceeded like this:

❖ I began with the Heart Opener.[7]

❖ I began my inquiry as the discomfort of my daughter's non-stellar academic performance arose. In this non-reactive space of witnessing awareness, I became curious about the feeling. Where was it? What did it feel like? It felt like a knot in the stomach area.

❖ Was the knot separate from the stomach? The knot wasn't *in* the stomach; it *was* the stomach. It arose and subsided.

❖ Was the stomach separate from the feeling of the knot? No. There was no stomach there and a feeling here. They arose as one.

❖ Was the feeling separate from witnessing awareness? No. Feeling as a sensory modality is awareness itself.

❖ Was there a separate feeler of this feeling? No. In direct experience, the feeling and the feeler are the same.

❖ Now I was curious about what I'd called the knot—anxiety. It was time to examine it. Did the feeling come with a label? No. It was just a sensation, not separate from witnessing awareness.

---

7. See Appendix p.163

❖ Did the word "anxiety" come up with the feeling of the knot? When I examined the word, I saw that it was an arising. When this word arose, the previous experience of the knot was no longer directly experienced. The knot had come and gone before the label "anxiety" arose.

❖ Did the label "anxiety" point to the knot? When I experienced the word, it was seen to be not separate from witnessing awareness, just as the feeling of the knot was. But wait. Another thought had risen claiming that the knot was anxiety.

❖ Did this claim-thought join the knot and the label? By the time it had risen, the knot and the label were no longer in my direct experience. The claim-thought was seen to be not separate from witnessing awareness.

❖ The knot, the label, and the claim-thought were all pointing to the same thing: witnessing awareness.

❖ The inquiry continued, moving to the story that my daughter "should" be a good student. Each story, thought, and belief examined in inquiry dissolves into witnessing awareness. As the inquiry deepened, another belief was uncovered—that her performance reflects mine as a parent.

❖ Could this parent be found? The feeling of the "I" arose. It was in the chest area. Was this "I" separate from witnessing awareness? No. Witnessing awareness was never not present, but the "I" came and went. It was an arising, like any other.

❖ Labels associated with the "I" were no different than labeling for the knot. Claim-thoughts arose independently, each an arising in witnessing awareness.

❖ As the inquiry continued, the stories of my daughter's imagined future arose. Every story of the past or the future arose in witnessing awareness *as* awareness, *now*. Every concept of success and failure arose as an arising. The labeling of arisings as "good," "bad," "desirable," or "undesirable" were additional, unrelated arisings brought together by claim-thoughts. No thought actually referred to another. Every thought and feeling always referred to awareness only.

❖ As the inquiry proceeded, the anxiety collapsed along with unquestioned assumptions, beliefs, and concepts. From the perspective of awareness, I saw that clarity gave way to peace and sweetness. There is great joy in seeing a delightful playfulness in this type of inquiry. Witnessing awareness stands everywhere, pouncing on us with a "Gotcha!"

In the love that emerges as a fruit of inquiry, my daughter was released from the tyranny of my "I," the competent parent. As the inquiry proceeded, it was clear that neither one of us, my daughter or I, is the body-mind entity of the default mode. [8]When I stand as awareness, she is me: vast, spacious, unlimited, unbounded joy and love with neither a past nor a future.

With this clarity, I talked to my family, asking that we back off and allow her to be. They complied, but reluctantly, since they believed that children must be pushed to realize their potential. We never said a word about this to her, but the

---

8. Default mode network: a brain network implicated in self-related thinking, mind wandering and being "on autopilot".

energy in the home had shifted from one of dissent to one of love and acceptance. I met her C grades with the same excitement and delight as her sister's A's. Being sensitive and intuitive, she began to blossom in this new environment. A few weeks later, she came home from school bursting with excitement: "Mommy, I got my first A in math!" We celebrated her joy. Overnight, she had transformed into the child we knew she was—curious, interested, and joyful about learning. Her grades improved steadily until she was getting straight A's.

Inquiry into the parent identity

We can inquire into beliefs about giving with wanting something back, such as success, our worth as parents, and so on. Every single time, we will come to see these concepts to be temporary arisings in witnessing awareness. They cannot be found to exist separately outside of awareness. Significantly, the "I" arises *as* the fear, the longing, and the pain. Again and again, we come to see that the "I" in its many forms of mental and emotional constructs is merely an arising. When we see this, the non-separation of the arising from the witnessing awareness becomes intuitively evident, and false identification is mitigated. We realize that we *are* awareness and that we are already complete and full. Suffering falls away and life becomes an outpouring of this fullness.

As our children begin to soak up this new paradigm of living, they can learn to give without fear. They can compete in academics, sports, and extracurricular activities without bitterness or rivalry. They can intuitively come to appreciate their friends without jealousy or one-upmanship. They can learn to question their own assumptions about reality and find freedom from suffering.

We don't inquire to gain a specific result with respect to our children, spouses, colleagues, or life situations. The purpose of inquiry is not to change our circumstances, but to examine our assumptions about them. Nothing in our lives may change as a result of inquiry, but nothing will seem quite the same when our assumptions dissolve. Although the situation with my daughter seemed to improve because of inquiry, such improvement is not always the result. When my children rebel, question my judgment, or undermine my suggestions, inquiry dissolves my assumptions that they "should" behave in certain ways. When I stand as awareness, I allow experience to arise as is, without manipulating it. In this allowing, the way I discipline my children also changes. I don't take their behavior personally; I can allow them to express themselves in unique ways even as I gently steer them away from harmful thinking and behaviors. Greg calls this delightful state of being "joyful irony."[9]

With joyful irony, I can be silly and flawed with my children because I don't take myself seriously either. They can watch me make a fool of myself, fall flat on my face, dance out of rhythm, or be spaced out. When I joyfully embrace these arisings in myself, they know it is okay for them to be perfectly flawed as well. When I release them from my ideas of perfection, they are free to embrace who they are evolving into. Most importantly, as I learn to stand as awareness, they can absorb the lesson that they are not limited beings meant to live cookie-cutter lives.

The direct path and real life

There can be a misunderstanding that inquiry leads to a paralysis of sorts, with the inability to take decisive action. In practice, however, successful inquiry results in increased energy and joyful harmony that guide our lives from within. This clear love helps us discipline children in intuitively loving and constructive ways, fostering greater intimacy and bonding.

9.   Goode, G. and Sander, T., *Emptiness and Joyful Freedom* and Goode, G., *The Direct Path: A User Guide*, see Reading List p.160

When our children come to understand that their behavior is not taken as a personal insult or threat by the parent, they gradually learn to behave in wholesome ways. When one of my daughters started middle school, she became increasingly argumentative and sassy. Her attitude began to annoy the whole family. When she pushed her limits one morning, I pulled her into a quiet room and asked her what was bothering her. She confessed that she was overwhelmed with homework and a rigorous school schedule that left her no time to relax every night. Together, we came up with a plan with which she could manage her time better. Soon she was less stressed, with a happier and more relaxed outlook. If I take her sassiness as a personal insult, I get caught up in defending my pride; I'm less likely to allow her to express herself freely. With the clarity of inquiry, I can allow her to discover who she is, without being threatened by her fluctuating moods.

The direct path doesn't dish out a fixed formula on how to live in the world and relate to other people. Parenting from the direct-path perspective doesn't look a certain way. When we see that labels don't really refer to anything but awareness, we discover the freedom of language and expression. When I talk to my children, I delight in how the concepts of happiness, success, college admissions, and job choices don't really refer to anything objective.

When my children rebel, throw temper tantrums, don't brush their teeth, or make poor choices for their health and well-being, I don't tell them it's okay because everything points to witnessing awareness! They are expected to follow the house rules about daily routines and habits, and face consequences for their actions. Yet, these rules are held lightly and joyfully, even when the children resent them and try to test their limits. I expect them to do their best according to their abilities, and to keep up their commitments, but neither their grades and trophies nor their failures and disappointments define me as a parent or entity. In inquiry, all concepts point to awareness, dissolving into joyful irony. When I hold their ups and downs lightly, they learn to take them in stride without pride, arrogance, or self-doubt. However, when arrogance, cattiness, or self-doubt arise (and they do), the children are guided in the moment by the clear love arising from inquiry.

I am sincere with my children when I tell them that they don't need to win my approval. I also tell them sincerely that I am (as a body-mind) severely flawed and that I don't really know all the answers. I thank them profusely on a daily basis for holding up a mirror to these flaws and for gracing my life with their divine presence.

Religion and the Direct Path
by Terry Moore

*" ... the direct path showed me that doctrine is not an end in
itself. But this new understanding of the place of experience in the
spiritual life is not simply an intellectual "Aha!" for me; it changes
the very substance of the spiritual path—or, at least, it does for
me. It has taken all the dead and brittle facts and doctrinal
principles I was already well acquainted with and breathed life
into them. The wisdom of the sages is no longer something to be
appreciated and learned and understood, but rather
something to be lived here and now."*

Introduction

When I found the direct path, I wasn't looking for a path; I
already had a path, and a good one. For more than 40 years
I have been a Perennialist and a member of a Sufi order, or
tariqah. So why would I look for anything more?

Over the last several years, I had begun to feel that that my
own practices had become too abstract and conceptualized,
and in many ways rote and dry. My discovery of the direct
path refocused my practices and helped me discover elements
that were lacking in my particular use and experience of them.
These were methodological keys that were not missing from
Sufism, but that had never been clear or actualized in my
own practice.

These keys and the perspective from which they came have
clarified and filled in much of the methodology of my Sufi
practice. My commitment to Sufism has been rekindled and
strengthened, and I have learned new ways of understanding
the prayers, invocation, and rituals that I have been doing for
years. The direct-path approach has given them light and life

15

and returned to me the wonder, joy, and enthusiasm for the sake of which I entered Sufism in the first place.

This ability of the direct path to enliven and illuminate the practice of Sufism surely extends to the practice of religion in general. In fact, the direct path and religion enhance each other: the direct path breathes life into the practice of religion, and the practice of religion prepares the heart for the direct path by clearing the road to the Absolute.

Perennialism and religion

This harmony between religion and the direct path is best understood from my own perspective not only as a Sufi, but also as a Perennialist. Perennialism goes by many names: Perennial Philosophy, Perennial Religion, *Sophia Perennis*, Traditionalism, and others. The root of the Perennialist perspective is the view that all of the world's religious traditions share a single, universal, and transcendent source and foundation. Perennialism is not a practice, but a lens through which the manifold religious and spiritual doctrines and practices of the world become intelligible according to their metaphysical source and means of transcending the personal in light of the Universal. This understanding is expressed in the title of Perennialist author Frithjof Schuon's famous book *The Transcendent Unity of Religions*.[10]

The importance of orthodoxy in practice

My own journey brought me to Perennialism before it brought me to Sufism. But, as I said above, Perennialism is not a practice, not a religion. Fortunately, the Perennialist authors I had discovered were very clear on the need for not only religious practice, but practice within an orthodox framework. I knew

---

10. Frithjof Schuon (1984) *The Transcendent Unity of Religions*, Quest Books, Wheaton, Illinois

most of the Perennialists I had been reading were attached to a Sufi *tariqah* that was not only Perennialist in its orientation but also orthodox in its practices.

This question of orthodoxy was, for me, extremely important in considering the choice of a spiritual path. I was seeking a path that, in the words of Frithjof Schuon, "participate[s], by way of a doctrine that can properly be called 'traditional,' in the immutability of the principles which govern the Universe and fashion our intelligence."[11] Although orthodoxy does not guarantee enlightenment, it is an extremely powerful means of protecting oneself from error. It was a great comfort to me to know that the path I was choosing had a long and honorable history and that it was not one person's idea or a newcomer on the scene.

Much of my feeling about the importance of orthodoxy comes from personal experience and contact with people who have had powerful mystical experiences. What is often problematic about these experiences is that those who have them have no greater context in which to situate what has happened to them. As a result, they end up making it up by themselves and trying to formulate from scratch a doctrine and method that can explain and recapitulate their own experience.

One cautionary tale of the hazards of mysticism without orthodoxy comes from my personal experience with someone I will call "Mr. Rose." Mr. Rose was a farmer from rural Ohio who had been overwhelmed by a powerful mystical experience one day on his tractor while planting soybeans. He struck me as an intelligent and sincere man, and he spoke with considerable conviction and charisma. By the time I went to meet him, he had collected a small clutch of young people around him who were pursuing the experience that he described with such great conviction. In addition to attending meetings at which he would

---

11. Polit, Gustavo trans. (1985) *Christianity/Islam: Essays on Esoteric Ecumenicism*, World Wisdom Books, Bloomington, Indiana

discuss his views, everyone in the group would spend so many hours a week driving a tractor, as Mr. Rose had been doing when he was overtaken by the experience. Tractor-driving was new to me as a mystical method.

Unfortunately, this story is rather typical in the history of mysticism. One can think of examples from classical and medieval times, yet there are examples even in the present day. In the 1960s, the band The Who produced the rock opera *Tommy*, which tells the story of just such a person and experience: a deaf, dumb, and blind boy who had a flash of enlightenment while playing pinball. Many acknowledged his "miracle" and sought to learn from him. He instructed them in the method that had worked for him, by giving his disciples eyeshades and earplugs and leading them to a pinball machine. But they were unable to have the same experience for themselves, and they ended up rejecting Tommy and his teaching. History is full of such stories; rarely is the music so good.

In the search for an authentic path, one often finds people like Mr. Rose, people who have had a powerful experience and now say they can teach you to transcend your own blindness and limitations so that you, too, can experience Reality/Illumination/Enlightenment/the Beatific Vision. But can they? How could you know? The problem is that even if Mr. Rose's experience is genuine, he cannot situate it in terms of a doctrine and method that is complete enough to be helpful to others. He has no comprehensive context in which to express who he is and what the world is, so he cannot convey the real breadth and depth of his experience. It is all too common for someone to have an individualized and fragmentary experience that he takes for full enlightenment, and it is a considerable limitation to his teaching if he has no access to the doctrinal and methodological resources that would make it easier to communicate to others.

This is a powerful argument for traditional orthodoxy. Sufism has had 1,500 years to work out and perfect its spiritual methodology. Buddhists claim 2,500 years of helping people to transcend the wheel of samsara. Finding a master of any kind is a serious undertaking, and the seeker needs to be as sure as possible of the master's credentials. Tradition and orthodoxy do not guarantee enlightenment, but they do greatly decrease the risk for the seeker of wasting his or her time or even life.

Religion has a long and proven history of bringing transcendent peace to countless millions and providing us with thousands of years of enlightened and realized sages and saints, most of whom made their journey to enlightenment in the context of religious practice. I suspect that virtually all those great lights would assert that their religious practice was essential to their journey to liberation and realization.

What can religion do for the direct path?

One of the remarkable things about the direct path is that its doctrine is so clear: awareness is everything, and all other things—objects, thoughts, feelings—are really just arisings in awareness. Period.

But how does the traveler absorb this simple truth? As all mystical travelers find out sooner or later, there is a difference between understanding a truth and realizing the truth in its full depth. A theoretical understanding of reality is insufficient; we must live the understanding and make it part of our own experience.

A conceptual understanding of reality is certainly necessary, and it can prompt and encourage the practice through which it becomes real knowledge. But relying only on conceptual knowledge can inhibit and truncate one's journey by substituting mere answers for the experiential response that questions need. Worst of all, a conceptual understanding can become simply a locus of identity and affiliation that gives travelers a sense of belonging to a kind of elite philosophy club that grants them an exalted status high and above the benighted souls who don't know the doctrine or speak its code words.

Conceptual knowledge may be a beginning, but the point is to make our knowing our being. It is precisely in this project that religion offers its assistance to the direct path. Every traditional and orthodox form contains doctrines and practices that facilitate the very objective the direct path offers so succinctly. Further, traditional religion gives the direct path a practice and environment in which to operate, highly useful tools, and a practical discipline that nurtures direct-path inquiry. In conjunction, tradition and the direct path form a kind of organic whole in which to live life and practice the path to awareness, liberation, enlightenment—whatever you want to call it.

Let me offer you an example from my own practice of Sufism of how religion can bring the truth offered by the direct path out of the realm of mere conceptual knowledge and into the life of the traveler. At the heart of Sufi practice is the *dhikr Allah*, the invocation of the great Name of God, Allah (literally "The God"). This kind of invocation is the same spiritual form of practice one finds throughout the world of mystical spirituality.

Other traditions know it by other names. It is the "prayer of the heart" of Christianity, the *nembutsu* of Buddhism, the *japa* of Hinduism. It is the technique of focusing the mind on a single sound or image and its repetition, which frees the mind from its constant circling and seeking of distraction. The very nature of the Name-sound-image, combined with the earnestness and intention of the practitioner, provides the power to liberate the separate self from its illusion of separate existence. The practice takes the doctrine of the direct path—that the separate existence of the self is an illusion—and allows it to be realized in the heart of the person who is invoking the Name.

In addition, the areas of practical life—especially matters of virtue and morality—are well covered by the great religious traditions, which now in the light of the direct path offer a comprehensive view of life while we are on the path of return to the source. It may be easy to see how compatible direct-path practice is with religion and traditional forms of spirituality, but it can be less clear how the direct path alone addresses the daily and practical issues that the religions deal with so specifically. Traditions offer a secure framework in which to make these decisions.

Another advantage of practicing a traditional form of religion—and this one is of particular importance for those who practice the direct path—is that traditional religion is a hedge against nihilism. It is all too easy to read some nondualist works that emphasize the point that personal agency does not exist, and conclude that there is no doer, no doing, and—consequently and necessarily—nothing to be done. This is one of those things that is true in principle but not in practice. By contrast, the direct path is all about practice, beginning and most fundamentally with the practice of doing self-inquiry. We all have to *do*. Our days are full of doing things. It cannot be otherwise. That being true, the question arises: *what* should I do? What is the *right thing* to do? Or, more fully presented: what *decisions* can I make? What *practices* can I take up that will facilitate my learning and knowing so that my theoretical knowledge of the truth of existence will become my experience and my lived reality? We are constantly presented with experiences that suggest we have a choice. We should intend the right thing and act accordingly. We should always choose that which makes the real more real to us, and the less real less real to us. We choose, and then we experience the result.

It is in this realm that traditional religion has much to offer the seeker in conjunction with the direct path. Religion and tradition are derived from the Ultimate Good and provide a context for living life and making the quotidian decisions of life easier by supplying a context and an attitude that conforms the seeker to the journey that he or she is taking. Religion and tradition supply points of reference for moral decision-making, which often relieves the stress of having so many things to decide. Further, they require a commitment on the part of the seeker, which weakens the false separate self by submitting it to that which is higher, more real, more true. They subordinate personal desire to divine Reality. They also prescribe for us attitudes for our understanding and our conduct, which are of critical importance for our journey. Our attitudes, according to the twentieth-century nondualist guru Nisargadatta,[12] are one of the few things we have any control over. Obviously, we should conform our attitudes to that which is most facilitative of our knowing the real.

What can the direct path do for religion?

I am a Sufi. Sufism is often defined as "Islamic mysticism." This is accurate, as it situates Sufism within the body of an orthodox tradition with all its formal practices, sacred history, religious and mystical scholarship, and wisdom traditions passed down through the generations. But after years of practice, I found that my own use of the method offered by my *tariqah* had become mechanical and ineffective. I was faithful to the practice but could not deny the feeling that my spiritual life had ceased to grow, that it was stalled and stale.

It was my discovery of the direct path that brought into my own practice the essential notion of examining my own experience. To my great surprise, there were many dimensions of the experience of invocation that I had never focused on or examined. The introduction of the notions of experience and inquiry has made every second of my practice rich and spiritually efficacious. Similarly, these direct-path concepts and methods have shed light on and given life to myriad spiritual and religious

12. Nisargadatta Maharaj, (2012) *I Am That*, The Acorn Press, Durham, NC.

practices that previously seemed obscure or even silly to me.

For example, one of the themes of meditation used in the invocation of the divine Name is the concept of transcendence—that God is perfect in His absoluteness, beside which we are nothing. This no longer seems like a philosophical or metaphysical axiom to this traveler, but a stage in the process of knowing the real. The point here is that we must first find out what we are not in order to find out what we really are.

The introduction of direct-path methods of inquiry has also added an element of interior spiritual guidance that had not been part of the milieu in which I learned this method. This lack was clearly a shortcoming. The direct path, with its emphasis on inquiry and the examination of experience, pointed the way for me to ask the questions that would make my own path live again.

There is a wonderful complementarity and harmony between Sufism and the direct path. With its emphasis on the primacy of experience, the direct path opens the meaning of what Sufism calls "tasting." Tasting is necessarily experiential and direct. This was the discovery that laid bare for me the value of the interrogation of personal experience. For example, one major change in my own practice has to do with presence. In Sufism, I have always understood the importance of being fully present in all the rites and activities. For the practices to be efficacious, one must be fully present. God demands all that we are, not simply our bodies or our minds reciting rote formulations. This kind of presence had always played an important role in my own practice. But now I see the rites and practices not as an occasion to make myself present, but as an occasion to remove my self and taste what is actually present. The effort is not to place myself into the practice but to get my self out of the way by focusing on the presence of the Real.

This has become my focus when I am in meditation, invocation, and sacred dance. Much language has been given to the notion of practicing the presence of God. But now it seems this way: the awareness of the presence of God is in fact the presence of the awareness of God. This discovery from the direct path has been essential in transforming my own practice from being about performance to being about awareness. And so the focus of my spiritual life has become more about the use of my attention and awareness than about performance. It has become more about being than about doing.

There is a great deal of literature and doctrine about the nature of the soul and its problems. Sufism provides complex descriptions of the different levels of the soul and its operation. Prior to my discovery of the direct path, many of these carefully worked-out explanations seemed like doctrine, that is, something to be learned and, perhaps, observed. But for the spiritual traveler, it is not enough to know the various aspects of the soul only in principle; they have to be experienced. The traveler needs to see each of them, along with their limitations, in action.

In this way the direct path showed me that doctrine is not an end in itself. But this new understanding of the place of experience in the spiritual life is not simply an intellectual "Aha!" for me; it changes the very substance of the spiritual path—or, at least, it does for me. It has taken all the dead and brittle facts and doctrinal principles I was already well acquainted with and breathed life into them. The wisdom of the sages is no longer something to be appreciated and learned and understood, but rather something to be lived here and now.

For example, one of the doctrines found throughout Islam and Sufism is a description of the soul, usually the "lower soul" with its various problems, opacities, passions, and errors. The Arabic term used for the soul is *nafs* (similar to the Hebrew *nephesh*, "animal spirit"). This is generally what the direct path and similar approaches refer to as the mind-body. This is the plane of battle for the greater holy war (*jihad al-akbar*). Sufism, similarly to other spiritual paths, can be described as a struggle with one's soul or a *jihad* with the *nafs*. I always thought I had understood this concept, and I took it in the context of this same battle from St. Paul: "I do not understand what I do. For what I want to do I do not do, but what I hate I do" (Romans 7:15).

Finally, thanks to the direct path, I understood that the effort (*jihad*) here is not to defeat the qualities of the soul. Defeating them would mean engaging them, which would give them more reality than they actually have. The effort is not to defeat the qualities of the soul, but rather to penetrate the illusion that they exist at all.

In providing instructions for carrying out this process, the direct path opened for me a key insight into the fundamental doctrine of my own religion. In Islam, the greatest sin is *shirk*, attributing partners to God. The fundamental principle of Islam is that there is only one God, and that He is "not begotten, not begetting, and that there is none comparable to Him" (Qur'an 112). So, if this is true, then who is this *nafs* that I must struggle against?

The direct path cleared this doubt about the *nafs* in a practical and useful way. This battle with the soul was not to engage it and tame it; rather the battle was to examine its qualities and behavior and determine what, if anything, it really was. Previously I had been all too willing to blithely go along in my spiritual practice and think that maybe someday I would come to know God. But this is a principal error that introduces dualism into a religion that is fundamentally an expression of divine unity. There isn't any "me and God"; there is only God.

The teaching about the *nafs* is just one example of the doctrines that are expressed in dualistic terms but can be—and must be—resolved to the One. For those who accept the basic doctrine of the faith, finally, there is no other conclusion possible.

Another key that the direct path has to offer traditional religions has to do with how to understand the place of religious experiences. Traditional religious practice tends to be dismissive of experiences, and understandably so, particularly for us children of the psychedelic era. The goal is to have a spiritual life, not a series of spiritual experiences. Tradition discourages centering the spiritual life around experiences, because the spiritual life is not about entertaining oneself, regardless of how lofty these experiences may be. The direct path opened my eyes to the proper place of experience in a clear and dramatic way, by showing me clearly first that tradition is right: experiences are beside the point; but at the same time—and this was what was so dramatic— that experience, as such, *is* the point. The roadblock *is* the gate. As Ibn 'Arabi says, the things that veil us from God are the very things He uses to reveal Himself to us. Experiences are irrelevant, but experience, as such, is the key.

The direct path takes experience as a starting point and calls into question what we previously accepted as knowledge, insisting that only the evidence provided by direct experience is reliable. At the same time, it gives the seeker full responsibility and assumes his competence—under the guidance of his teacher—to learn the discernment required to verify the truth of the teachings. The direct path's process is to perform the experiment to "see for yourself" rather than simply to believe. The only fundamental belief, which must at least be present as an intuition, is the sole reality of the One. The direct path thus gives the seeker tools for bringing what begins as a detached, merely intellectual belief into his or her immediate experience. These direct-path keys that have so enriched my practice of Sufism are available to other traditional religions as well.

Harmony between religion and the direct path

Religion is more than just a finger pointing at the moon. Each authentic tradition speaks to the whole of the person, to the spirit and the soul and the body, and by bringing all of these levels of the microcosm into play—by providing doctrine for the mind, moral precepts for the will, objects of devotion for the sentiment, and ritual for the body—it serves to protect us against the hypertrophy or deviation of any one of these levels. Seen through the direct-path lens, all of these things become operative tools for learning and growing. In this way, religion enhances the direct path, and the direct path enhances religion.

For these reasons, it is clear that there is a great possibility for synthesis and harmony between the direct path and the practice of traditional religion. I have experienced this harmony in my own practice. More than once, I have heard experienced direct-path teachers comment that students from a structured background seem to do better in the direct path than those from non-believing or non-practicing backgrounds. We certainly come here as we are. But once we have arrived here, it would seem that a strong traditional practice in light of and in conjunction with the direct path provides the most efficacious choice for life and path.

Similarly, I have known several men and women who adhere strongly to their traditional faith and have discovered the direct path. None have considered leaving their tradition. All have given thanks to God for the advent in their lives of the direct path approach. Traditional practice, with its insistence on goodness, honor, compassion, generosity, and the other virtues, provides a kind of holistic Royal Road to the Absolute.

Confessions of an Experience Junkie
by Steve Diamond

*"I confess I have no fixed answer. All I seem to know
is the beauty of the journey."*

I was an experience junkie, and this is my story.

What is an experience junkie? Someone who hungers for, searches after, and collects specific varieties of experience. In the context of a spiritual path, it's a student who feels that his or her attainment is contingent on and measured by a collection of mystical experiences or blissful experiences or whatever kind of experiences seem most important. In extreme cases, like mine, it can mean an insatiable craving for these experiences.

When I say "experiences" I'm including the related idea of states—states of mind or states of consciousness. For the purposes of this chapter, I would say that the difference between an experience and a state is simply that a state lasts longer. So a spiritual experience junkie may be someone seeking extended blissful states, or extended states of "being fully present," or whatever desirable states they've conceptualized and imagined as the ultimate attainment. They're likely also to believe that transient peak experiences can be extended into permanent states.

A peak experience

"This is the path of self-realization, not a summer camp!" This was my voice booming across the parking lot and catching some latecomers by surprise.

It was 3:15 on a fine summer afternoon in the lake district of Muskoka, a two-hour drive north of Toronto. The year was 1976, and the difficulty was that the check-in time for that week's spiritual retreat had been designated as 3:00. That's why I was bellowing.

This sort of behavior was well outside my norm, which tends to be gentle and mild-mannered. What had given me not just the confidence but also the arrogance to address my fellow spiritual students so rudely? Therein lies a tale.

I had arrived at the lakeside residential retreat two weeks earlier. It was my first spiritual retreat of any kind. I'd never met most of the other students.

One custom was that before dinner, which the students ate together in a large dining hall, someone would offer a recitation from our teacher's words. The first week of the summer there were only about two dozen students present. My fourth evening there, I volunteered to recite from memory a paragraph from the lecture the teacher had given a few days previously. It was the first time I'd done anything of the kind, and I was a little nervous. But I'd practiced quite a bit and felt reasonably confident I could pull it off.

I stood and began to speak. My recitation started smoothly, but after a couple of sentences I stopped abruptly. My mind had gone entirely blank. I don't just mean I'd lost the thread of the words. I had. But more than that, there was no thought whatever. My mind was empty and open and still. Never before or since have I experienced anything quite like it.

As I stood there waiting for something to happen, a surge of energy arose. It felt like it was pushing me through a doorway into another place. After 10 seconds or so the words returned and I continued, with a considerably altered experience and perspective.

Here's an inventory of the changes I noticed, no doubt edited in memory during the intervening 40 years:

1) Heightened intensity of perception, meaning bright colors, distinct sounds, intensified touch.

2) Little need for sleep. I'd rest a few hours at night, but it didn't seem much like sleep. I was aware most of the time.

3) A very cool and clear mental state, untroubled by thoughts. Not an absence of thoughts, but rather a different perspective on them. I felt and visualized that I occupied a position on top of a tall cliff overlooking the ocean. Thoughts would originate way down below, rise toward me, and dash themselves into oblivion against the cliff before they reached me.

It was the third aspect that really grabbed me. There was a sense of total peace and clarity, and the absence of any sort of mental conflict or distress. My point of view was above all that, naturally and spontaneously.

I thought, "I'm enlightened! I have achieved my spiritual ambition! This must be what it's like: full and permanent enlightenment!"

I was mistaken. Three days later the experience ended. The state left as suddenly as it had arrived. I was bereft.

Let's take a step back to explore where I'd acquired my notion of "full and permanent enlightenment" and why I was fixated on it. After all, where there are junkies there must be pushers.

Birth of a junkie

Like many teenagers growing up in the 1960s (or any other time), I was troubled. I was an academic whiz in high school, but socially awkward. I had a strong and persistent sense that school wasn't answering any of the really important questions. I wasn't sure exactly what those questions were—perhaps "What is a good life?" and "What is true happiness?"—but I knew they weren't being discussed in front of me. At times I even imagined a conspiracy of adults to keep certain topics hidden from youngsters.

My parents were no help. When I asked them why they never talked about the big questions, they said, "Oh, we don't have to discuss philosophy. We did that years ago and we already know how we feel." I found that absurd. They'd settled questions the great philosophers had been discussing for thousands of years? Ridiculous!

For me, this philosophical unrest got combined with an acute and painful psychological unrest. Away from home for my freshman year of college, I experienced near-paralysis due to anxiety and depression. I had to drop out, and eventually to seek help in the form of psychotherapy.

I don't think the therapy ever made a lot of difference. I outgrew the adolescent angst sufficiently to become a working adult within a few years. But I wasn't very happy, and the philosophical unrest remained also. They'd gotten blended.

Cue the pushers.

(Now, please don't take me too literally here. When I mention specific people—authors and teachers—I'm not accusing them of deliberately and maliciously pushing harmful and addictive concepts onto a pliable and susceptible public, the way drug pushers do. I am saying there are certain parallels. Draw your own conclusions.)

When I reached my early 20s, I encountered a group of recently published books that spoke directly to my frustration and yearning. The first was *The Book: On the Taboo Against Knowing Who You Are*, by Alan Watts.[13] I'd never before heard the message that we aren't really who we think we are and the world isn't really what we think it is. At last here was someone talking about the taboo I'd intuited as a teen! I felt grateful and relieved.

---

13. Watts, Alan (1966) *The Book: On the Taboo Against Knowing Who You Are*, Pantheon Books, New York

The second book, the one that really calibrated my intentions, was *The Master Game: Beyond the Drug Experience*,[14] by Robert S. de Ropp. In it, he observes that different people choose to play the game of life for different rewards. Among those popular in Western society are wealth, power, and fame. But, he argues, the only reward really worth playing for is higher consciousness, spiritual awakening, because it erases the reliance on any other reward for one's feeling of fulfillment.

This passage gives the flavor:

> [The Master Game] remains the most demanding and difficult of games and, in our society, there are few who play…. The aim of the game is true awakening, full development of the powers latent in man. The game can be played only by people whose observations of themselves and others have led them to a certain conclusion, namely, that man's ordinary state of consciousness, his so-called waking state, is not the highest level of consciousness of which he is capable. Once a person has reached this conclusion, he is no longer able to sleep comfortably. A new appetite develops within him, the hunger for real awakening, for full consciousness.

Let's pause and notice something about the writing. It uses terms like "true awakening," "real awakening," and "full consciousness" as if they literally refer to a phenomenon that can be pinned down, defined, and recognized, and that it's reasonable to assert someone has or hasn't attained. It's no wonder that this language encourages hunger! As we'll come to see later, we are not compelled to talk about the goals of spiritual practice in such terms.

---

14. De Ropp, Robert S. (1968) *The Master Game: Beyond the Drug Experience*, Delacorte Press, New York

But I didn't know that at the time. I took the language very literally indeed. I took it to heart. I developed that appetite. I didn't know how I was going to fulfill it, but the hunger was there.

Chasing states

Within three or four years, I met my first spiritual teacher. It was at his summer retreat that I believed I'd achieved enlightenment, only to be devastatingly disappointed three days later.

My thoughts at the time went along these lines: *when I'm in the presence of the teacher, I get a fantastic high-energy buzz. I feel electrified, alive.* I almost grasped real enlightenment, but it eluded me. Therefore, what I must do is stay as close to the teacher as I can, as often as I can, and collect more of these experiences. One day it's going to be permanent. This must be how it works.

There's one enormous flaw in that line of reasoning, one that was pointed out by Chögyam Trungpa in his 1973 book, *Cutting Through Spiritual Materialism.*[15] It's this: when we chase experiences and states, no matter how pleasant or exalted, they inevitably end. And when they do, we suffer the pain of loss. We suffer it over and over again. We end up worse off than we'd have been had we never experienced the bliss or the peace or whatever it was. We suffer more, not less.

It's like any type of addiction, including drugs. The euphoria of the high can't compensate for the despair of the low. The addict always comes down, always has to search for the next fix.

In my case this search consumed me for 25 years.

Oh, I had a career, I had relationships, but my overriding goal was always "real awakening," and I felt that if only I could get close enough to the teacher, often enough, for long enough, I'd reach it.

---

15. Trungpa, Chögyam (1973) *Cutting Through Spiritual Materialism,* Shambhala Publications, Boulder

At the same time, the fixes I got from seeing him, in the form of euphoric and blissful states, both sustained me and kept me enslaved. I always craved another. Even though it became pretty obvious at some point that they were always going to be temporary, I kept coming back.

I want to say clearly and emphatically that the dysfunctional dynamic was purely of my own making. I don't blame the teacher. In fact, he told me repeatedly that my infatuation with his presence and with what he called secondary effects of his teaching (meaning euphoria, energy states) was highly detrimental. I simply didn't hear, didn't understand, or couldn't act on that advice.

On the path

Eventually I broke away, eventually the teacher died, and thus I entered a long fallow period, about 10 years, when I hardly thought of spiritual paths at all.

When my interest revived, I was fortunate to encounter the direct path and some people who studied it and practiced this approach under Greg Goode's guidance. However, I brought to it the same addictive tendencies I'd lived out before. This is the story of how they dissolved.

Or maybe not so much *how*. It's a story, and the tendencies dissolved, but to some extent the *how* remains mysterious.

The direct path presents a systematic approach, certainly. But it would be a mistake to extrapolate that each student proceeds along the path in a linear, systematic fashion. No—or at least that's not my experience. There are fits and starts and missteps, loops and curlicues and spirals. There are repeated returns to the same questions, each visit bringing different insights. Above all, there are changes in perspective, attitude, and affect that just seem to happen. If you asked me to say which step, which insight, caused a particular change, I couldn't do it. And I don't have to, I'm glad to say!

I'm reminded of a simile used by one teacher I know. He says being a spiritual student is like when you wake up in the morning with a headache. You dress, have breakfast, and go about your day. At some point you realize your headache is gone. You don't know when or how it went; you just know it's gone. Much of my experience with the direct path is like that.

Disclaimer: what I say here about the direct path is my own experience and interpretation of it. It's apt to disagree in spots with anyone else's version. This is a good thing! It's a living teaching.

The direct path provides a framework and a set of tools for investigating our actual experience as it is, not as we believe it to be.

Here's a simple example, the experience of hearing. We've been taught to believe hearing works like this: An object in the external world vibrates and emits a sound, which takes the form of vibrations in the air. When these sound waves reach our eardrums, they cause the eardrums to vibrate. Through the mechanisms of our middle and inner ears, the waves are transformed into nerve impulses that our brains interpret as sounds.

I'm not going to give the details of the investigation here. They're in Greg's books,[16] among other places. The short version is that when we look closely at the actual experience of hearing, setting aside what we've been taught, we find none of that complexity. We find no sound waves, no ears, no brains. We find no distinction between an internal and an external world. We find no object emitting a sound. In fact we don't even find a sound! All we find is the experience of hearing. And we don't even really find hearing. In essence we find only the awareness that knows hearing.

Through a series of such investigations, we uncover the truth of our own actual experience as it's always been, freed

16. See Reading List p.160

from the accretion of layers of education and cultural conditioning. Gradually our erroneous beliefs fall away until we stand revealed as what we were all along: consciousness, awareness its very self.

Notice that this approach is the diametric opposite of the one implied by, for instance, the excerpt from *The Master Game*. There's no concept of an ultimate state to attain ("real awakening"), along with which the student will automatically and magically come to know the truth. No. The truth is already what we are. It's what we experience at every moment. To see it clearly we only need to change what we believe ourselves and our experience to be.

Challenges

But did I begin my journey on the direct path with this understanding? Hell, no! I began it with my prior tendencies intact: my belief in an ultimate state and my yearning for blissful experiences. This led me to confront a number of obstacles.

One obstacle came in the form of an exercise called The Heart Opener.[17] It's presented as a prelude to each of the investigations, and it uses guided imagery to remind us of our nature as awareness and to suggest that the taste of sweetness and a sense of spaciousness characterize that remembrance.

Fine and dandy. But two groups of questions arose for me. One, what if it fails to induce a feeling of sweetness and spaciousness? Does that mean there's something wrong? And two, when it does seem to induce a feeling of sweetness and spaciousness, what's the point? Does it mean I'm any closer to really awakening? How could it, when it's obviously a temporary state?

So I'd feel dissatisfied when The Heart Opener didn't seem to be working as intended, and I'd also feel dissatisfied when it did.

---

17. See Appendix p.163

Let's look more closely at each instance. At first I thought that when there was no feeling of sweetness and spaciousness, I must be doing something wrong. I still subscribed to a model of linear, progressive improvement. If the student performs the right tasks correctly, the reward will be enlightenment. If not, the reward will never arrive.

That's the junkie's attitude. Something is lacking and something must be done to remedy the lack. The direct path begins with a different premise. We are already at home in our true identity as unlimited awareness. We may not fully realize or understand that yet, but there's nothing we can do, there can't possibly be anything we can do, that would change what we are. Nothing is truly lacking. As I began to understand this, the fear of getting it wrong began to dissipate.

The other case is more instructive. When temporary sweetness and spaciousness are experienced, what's the point? A junkie would say, "Give me more," but that wasn't working for me by this time. I'd recognized that no temporary phenomenon was magically going to become permanent. So how was I to understand the Heart Opener? And more generally, how was I to understand the everyday experience of a sense of sweetness coming and going with no apparent cause or reason?

See, within a year or less after starting the direct path, I began to notice regular visitations (experiences) of what I call a sense of extreme wellbeing. I can't be sure it's exactly the same thing the teaching calls sweetness, but I'm pretty sure it's closely related. It certainly feels sweet, like a warm embrace.

These visitations generally last a couple of minutes. Sometimes more, sometimes less. Occasionally there may be an obvious trigger, like when the cat jumps onto my lap and purrs. But more often they just come over me without warning. One venue that seems especially conducive happens to be the grocery store. The other day I found myself dancing and singing along with the tune on the loudspeaker, all in the middle of the produce section! I have no explanation for this.

Naturally, I wanted to know the significance of these experiences. Some teachers say these are moments when the clouds of ignorance that distract us from the truth clear temporarily, and we see the truth directly. Others say these temporal, phenomenal experiences are at most reminders of or metaphors for the peace and sweetness of our true nature. Those views aren't exactly compatible. Is one right and one wrong?

I found the direct seeing idea attractive. The warm embrace was coming from unlimited awareness itself. I was directly touched by the truth of being.

This sounded good to me at first. But I soon saw several problems in the light of the direct path. For one thing, it's a dualistic view. It has me separate from awareness, experiencing it from afar. It implies that I'm a limited being progressing toward a distant goal. Worse (from a junkie's perspective), it makes these transient experiences into important goals: "If only I could have more of these, if I could have them continuously, I'd really have arrived."

I already knew that wasn't the way, and I turned toward the metaphorical interpretation. I'll have more to say about that a little later.

Presence and preferences

What finally started the dissolution of the junkie was close contemplation of another experience I'd brought from my earlier life. The first few meetings I'd had with my first spiritual teacher were small and informal. Three or four of us would be sitting at his feet, and we'd chat about everything under the sun. At intervals, he'd unexpectedly extend a leg, aiming a playful kick in my direction.

Doesn't sound like much, does it? I didn't think so either at the time. I only made the connection years later. But apparently it affected my daily experience deeply, because I began to notice multiple times a day a conscious jolt of transition. It seemed I'd moved from an everyday state of consciousness to one that was somehow more aware. I thought of it as waking up, "coming to," with an associated image of snapping fingers because it was quick and abrupt.

I also correlated it with a list I'd seen in de Ropp's book, *The Master Game*. He lists five levels of consciousness:

1) Deep sleep without dreams.

2) Sleep with dreams.

3) Waking sleep (identification).

4) Self-transcendence (self-remembering).

5) Objective consciousness (cosmic consciousness).

In this scheme, level three is the everyday waking state. Level four is a step beyond, but still short of enlightenment. I believed I was feeling, repeatedly, the jolt of waking up from level three to level four. Hallelujah! I was becoming more awake.

I took this interpretation so seriously that I devised a way to induce the transitions more frequently. I got a sheet of adhesive stickers illustrating butterflies, and I stuck them in places I encountered frequently: the bathroom mirror, the refrigerator, the typewriter. (Yes, this was a long time ago, and I was at university. The typewriter got lots of use!) The idea was that when I saw a butterfly, I'd remember to wake up.

It worked, a little, for three or four days. After that the novelty wore off. They were no longer unexpected, just part of the everyday environment. The transitions persisted, and gradually they became less abrupt.

Many years later, after I began following the direct path, I learned a new vocabulary for describing these transitions, which I continued to notice daily. The description came from the secular mindfulness movement. It divides our experience into intervals when we're on autopilot, not paying much attention to what's going on, and intervals when we're "mindfully present," more immediately aware of where we are and what we're doing. In the mindfulness practices, generally speaking the goal is to spend less time on autopilot and more time mindfully present.

Is this starting to sound familiar? Yup, it's yet another way of elevating one kind of experience over another, another way of encouraging an experience junkie to seek the one and avoid the other.

So how did the direct path help me break the pattern? Very simply by pointing out that my true nature, limitless awareness, is always already present regardless of any states, levels, or specific experiences. What I am is that which is never not present.

In the light of that idea, I really looked at those moments of transition, the moments when I seemed to wake up, to "come to." Right after each transition, I had the sense that "I wasn't very present before and now I am," or "I was sleepwalking, on autopilot, and now I'm awake." But when I looked, when I really looked, I saw that I'd never truly experienced a discontinuity in awareness. I'd never experienced my own absence (that would be impossible!), and I could use memory to see that I'd actually known what was going on before the transition just as well as after. I found no evidence the transition experiences truly had the meaning I'd been giving them.

Repetition and remembrance of this discovery whittled away my tendency to prefer one state to another. The notion that I was ever or could ever be *not* fully present stopped making sense. And this calming of opposites, this dissolution of dualities, began to extend into other areas. This appeared, for instance, as a broadening of preferences. I like more kinds of music, more genres of fiction, more kinds of art.

Obviously I still have likes and dislikes. It would be mighty hard to navigate everyday life without preferences. Every time you opened a restaurant menu, you'd get stuck and have to ask someone to order for you!

But I take my preferences more lightly, less literally and seriously. I don't have to have chocolate ice cream tonight. Lemon sorbet would be nice too. I don't have to listen to Mozart. You'd rather hear the Beatles? Fine with me. And I've stopped longing for peak experiences like the highs I had with my teacher. They never had anything to do with the truth of being. They were distractions.

Seen in this light, even the metaphorical interpretation of the sweet visitations I mentioned doesn't seem overly compelling. Like all other specific experiences, they come and they go. If I'm told that they symbolize the true "peace that passeth all understanding," what does that really add to my knowledge? How is it helpful? As far as I can tell, it's not. I can still enjoy those experiences when they occur without giving them special significance. If I felt an inclination to attach to them because they're so very pleasant, then the metaphorical interpretation could help that preference to subside. Otherwise, it seems unnecessary.

And so it goes

This is how life continues to flow. Distinctions that were once taken very seriously, like seeker vs. teacher, or unenlightened vs. enlightened, lose their sting. They subside to unimportance or even to comedy.

You may be wondering at this point why I'm still describing my life and measuring my so-called "attainment" according to an experience-based yardstick, while claiming at the same time to have outgrown the experience junkie character. That is, I'm still talking about how experience feels to me rather than about transcending experience entirely and entering a realm of pure knowledge, or something of the sort.

It's a good question, and I feel the best answer is the entire story. I've tried to convey a changed relationship with experiences and states, one that's gentler and freer, that lacks the junkie's cravings and obsessions. You'll be the judge of whether the story makes sense.

You may also be asking what I see now as the endpoint of the path, now that "true awakening" and "full consciousness" have failed the test of truly referring to anything meaningful.

That's a good question too. I confess I have no fixed answer. All I seem to know is the beauty of the journey.

The Windows in My Head
by Zachary Rodecap

"I have been brought to a special place by the direct path approach, but it is not yet the vista of all-is-awareness. A very powerful tool has been placed in my hands, one that bids me, more than any I've encountered, to look right now at my direct experience. For in it is already the liberation from all teachings."

Discovering assumptions

Having spent the better part of the last 15 years with my nose buried in sundry nonduality books, I approached *The Direct Path: A User Guide*[18] with a balanced mixture of old-hand confidence—*I've got this*—and world-weary fatigue—*I've probably seen this before.* My attitude could have been best summed up as the antithesis of Suzuki Roshi's *Zen Mind Beginner's Mind*[19] approach. This was more like sarcastic-high-schooler's-eye-rolling mind (a very secret teaching, that one).

Still, what led me to it, even after 15 years of accomplished seeking, was a vivid, even urgent, yearning to see through the story of a separate self. There was even a hint of desperation in my approach to the book, a kind of last-ditch, Hail-Mary attempt to finally just "get it." But I was in for a surprise. Not only would I not "just get it," but the book, and the path, would reveal that many of my underlying assumptions had gone entirely unquestioned. They were functioning in the background, like malware, possibly disabling my better attempts to "make progress."

Curiously, one of these assumptions was the objectivist-materialist worldview (I say "curiously" because one might assume

18. See Reading List p.160
19. Suzuki, S. (2005) *Zen Mind, Beginner's Mind*, Shambhala Publications, New York

43

that after 15 years of self-identifying as a nondualist, I would have long since given up such assumptions). So fundamental had objective materialism become to my identity that it was my unquestioned meta-narrative, the preferred vocabulary against which all things were to be measured. In another way, it was my security and comfort. That it might have been working against the very insights I was yearning for was a possibility I'd never considered—that is, until my worldview, which I regarded as eloquently based in nondualism, came under the scrutiny of the direct path, especially as presented by Greg Goode in his writings.

This is the story of the turbulence that ensued during the collision between a narrative I took to be true (that I am a nondualist) and the narrative that was actually true (that I still held fiercely to objective materialism). But this story, were it framed as cinema, would be French in nature, for it has no tidy ending. It ends *in medias res*.

Escape from one objectivism to another

Like most people's path to nonduality, mine has been circuitous. I was fervently evangelically Christian in my teens, and deeply embedded in this worldview was an objectivist viewpoint that became, as I can see now, the template for any metaphysical evaluation I made from that point forward. There was Truth and there were Truth claims, and through an honest reliance on reason and rationality, one could make objective statements as to how closely these two entities were related, and then make adjustments to the claims as needed.

Under the sway of objectivism, I believed, then, that the only escape from a false worldview was to replace the false narrative with a true one. The coexistence of two worldviews was a logical impossibility. Thus, like the 'droids escaping from Darth Vader's clutches, I used the escape-pod of science and materialism to make my own getaway from the Empire of Christendom.

Yet, in so doing I added an additional layer of certainty to objectivity: now, thanks to science, I could be sure that I was at least provisionally right. Seeing my liberation from what I considered to be the superstitions of Christianity as a gift of Rationality, I deeply vowed to never let go of that tool (as if it were a life raft). If I was not vigilant, I feared that I would somehow be seduced back into the warm somnambulism of belief again. At any rate, all subsequent shifts in worldview followed that template: the false was replaced with the true, and when the new arrived, the old was rather unceremoniously discarded.

Zen and the separate self

When I finally came to practice Zen, with a decidedly secular approach, I found (in retrospect) the materialist mindset to be oddly unchallenged and even supported, though this likely reflects my own misunderstanding of the tradition. While Zen philosophically posits the Absolute and the relative, most of the emphasis (particularly in the schools I was involved in) was on the relative perspective, the perspective in which there are existing individuals, who are products of evolutionary forces and made up of psychological layers of containment, and who, through meditation practice, come to see (either through a gradual progression or a sudden event) that there is actually no self and that all things are empty.

So my approach was to simply accept material reality as it appeared, while nurturing the belief that eventually I would see through it. And seeing through the story of the separate self would be an event, one that would arise as a kind of perceptual explosion, always in the future. But there were no traces of that reality in my current experience.

While I always bought into the view that there is no separate self, I didn't realize that the foundation of that statement also implied its logical corollary: there is no other self either.

Somehow, I think I'd constructed a metaphysics in which the only non-existing entity in the world was *myself*; objects, I took for granted. The not-two reality that all the great traditions pointed to was, in the end, perhaps some kind of a mythic energy connection between all beings.

Advaita and nonduality

I did, however, become an eclectic student of Zen, and came to incorporate a wide spectrum of teachers into my tool belt. In pretty short order, I eventually read my way to Advaita[20] and nonduality and felt a live connection to it. But so deeply embedded were my materialist assumptions that even the implications of the teachings of Ramana Maharshi[21] and Sri Nisargadatta[22]—steadfast in the Advaitic pointing to the primacy and transcendence of consciousness—were, when I read and consulted them, almost invisible to me. I simply took the concept of the "Self" and translated it into "non-self," deciding that everyone was pointing to the same thing anyway.

But my contact with Advaita and nonduality was deeply compelling—especially my reading of the *Ashtavakra Gita*,[23] which spoke to something that aligned with my experience: that there is *something* changeless against which the kaleidoscopic world of experience plays out. I could sense this "something" as a substratum of all my experience. I could even trace it backwards to my time as a child. It felt familiar, kind—closer

---

20. Advaita: from the Sanskrit "not two"
21. Ramana Maharshi 1879-1950. *Nan Yar - Who Am I?* Open Sky Press. (2015 edition)
22. Nisargadatta Maharaj(1999) *I Am That: Talks with Sri Nisargadatta Maharaj* (S D Dikshit [ed]) Revised edition (1999) Chetana Private Ltd.
23. *Ashtavakra Gita*: a classic Advaita Vedanta work, widely available in translation

than myself in some strange way. I wanted a way to resolve my Zen practice with this new vocabulary—and there are many teachers who do so—but I was tiring of Zen practice itself. It had this classical disciplinarian approach to spiritual practice that I was moving away from energetically.

Discovering awareness

At some point, though, surprisingly right when I was ready to really re-commit myself to a more formal lay practice of Zen, my energy for it simply evaporated. It vanished, almost overnight, and I found myself wandering, as many a seeker will do, into the receding horizon that is the satsang universe of YouTube. In it, I made my way somehow to the stream of videos by Rupert Spira and found an immediate connection with what he says: awareness —rather than the clunky, effortful mindfulness-hybrid I'd concocted—was always, already present, effortlessly. It couldn't be any other way.

Not only that, but "I" was this ever-present, clear, and pristine awareness and I didn't have to develop it through Jedi-like mind training and lotus-position devotion. And everything I perceived (through an alchemy I didn't quite understand but chose to believe anyway) was also already this awareness. Most important, if I really looked into my own experience, carefully, without the addition of memory or inference, I would actually perceive this truth, perhaps through a perceptual shift. The important thing was that this wasn't a future-event-oriented substantiation; it was to be had right here and now, through careful inquiry. Even the idea itself—that I was effortlessly the awareness in which all things appeared—was profoundly restful.

I was hooked. In the ever-updating palimpsest that was my understanding of literal truth, the direct path (I was still unaware of its moniker, though) was written on top: it was replacing all that had come before it as the best account of reality. The objective scientist was still ever alive and well. And, truthfully, as what the Buddhists might call a "useful means," the direct path was serving a deeply felt need, in that it was speaking to personal concerns I had about my approach to inquiry, which had previously only been informed by Ramana Maharshi's approach. I was beginning to integrate these tools into my interpretation of experience, particularly the insight (though this is not unique to the direct path) that I was awareness, and everything I could perceive—including mind, body, thoughts, feelings and perceptions—was an object of, and simultaneously one with, awareness.

Encountering the direct path

I clearly wanted more, though, and if you ask, the internet provides, which is how I found myself on a Facebook group devoted to supporting and guiding readers of *The Direct Path: A User Guide.*[24] It is important to relate, though, that while I was now a member of this group, I still had not read (nor did I even own) the source text. My experience with formally investigating my experiences was limited to a few guided yoga meditations on YouTube, and while I thought I understood the point, I didn't really grasp the detail or the methodology, which is why I was in for a bit of a surprise.

While all the hallmarks of the direct path as I'd come to know it through Rupert Spira were visible, there was a philosophical rigor in this approach that was totally unexpected. I'd ask a question on the group page and see, in some cases, the assumptions it was based on entirely deconstructed before my eyes. A comment I'd make that might presume the existence of the body-as-feeler would be questioned by some user, and I'd be left dumbfounded: *What on earth do you mean by questioning the existence of my hand?*

24. See Reading List p.160

The direct path: enticing, rigorous... and confusing

Here is where the water began to get a bit choppy. I felt riveted by the observations folks were making about facts I took as givens, yet I couldn't divine from what framework these statements arose, and the fact that it was users (not published nonduality authors) who were making many of these statements—making them *as their own*, not second-hand regurgitations—that fact began to both inspire *and* infuriate me. I had to understand this framework, this model. It was too counter-intuitive not to be enticing. It was harder than a nut to crack, yet it exuded some juiciness that was seductive. I had to see it for myself. There was something subversive and rigorous about *The Direct Path: A User Guide*. It was inviting and kind, yet it was coming from some place I couldn't identify—there was a playful rigor that was entrancing.

Into my Amazon cart went the *The Direct Path: A User Guide*, and, three weeks later (I live in Seoul, South Korea), into my hands it came. But, as I mentioned earlier, I wasn't exactly in a beginner's mind-mood when I received the book. I speed-read through massive quantities of the text, dipping into the experiments with the randomness of a child at a buffet, yet expecting (urgently hoping for) perceptual explosions to occur at any moment. The speed with which I approached the text belied one simple truth: the more I read, the more stunned I became that I actually didn't understand a thing. And yet I couldn't admit it to myself. There were whole paragraphs that I read in utter confusion, the total confusion of listening to the news in a foreign language. But I mercilessly suppressed the interior voice that alerted me to the fact.

Take, as a small illustration, this passage: "[T]he only way to verify the independent existence of a color is to visually experience a color that is present but unseen and to then verify that vision actually sees that same color" (p. 34). On first reading,

I pretended that the meaning of that was as clear as a grocery list, but the truth is it stuck in my craw like a sideways bone, because I was actually thinking, "There's no way that makes *any* sense. What on earth is an unseen color?" Passage upon passage piled up like this one, until I began wondering—genuinely—if there was a *The Direct Path: A User Guide for Dummies* available. (Perhaps I've found my calling.)

Yet, here I am. And here I'll stay, until or unless Sri Krishna Menon himself comes and excuses me, with a kindly gesture that says, "Enough, enough now."

A rock in my shoe

It is important at this point to defuse any anticipation the reader might have—based on countless prior templates—that this essay will end with a satisfying *dénouement*. None is to be had here, as I mentioned in the introduction. This is a story of getting a rock stuck in my shoe, a rock I can't shake out. All paths are temporary tools, and the direct path, to me, is right now like a new romantic lover, one whom you cinematically embrace in one moment and then ignore at a café the next. But while there will be no explosions, ice melts slowly, and perhaps that is my path: the slowly-melting-ice-with-a-rock-in-the-shoe Way™.

Two windows in my face

But I do want to share a few things that have shaken loose (besides my wits) in the course of these experiments. Not insights, per se, just place-markers I have noted. Perhaps they can be signposts for those who come behind, particularly those of the materialist-objectivist persuasion.

One of the first absurdities that occurred to me in the course of the experiments was that I truly believed—in contradiction to what even conventional science says—that my sensory apparatus didn't present a *representation* of the world; it presented the world *as it is*. For instance, I conceived of visual data as coming to me through two windows in my face. If I had wanted to feel sophisticated, I might have described them as lenses (they could, after all, focus), but for all practical purposes, there was, in my mental model, nothing representational happening: the world is as the world is seen. This applied to all my senses. All the scientific or philosophically based models of perception presented in *The Direct Path* (like naïve realism) were totally news to me.

So, how is it possible to look afresh at your sensations—to look afresh at the conditioned conclusions based on those sensations—when you're completely sure that what you perceive *is* the world itself? If my self were a little man looking out through those windows in my face, and if, additionally, he were able to jump outside my head (like getting out of a car), I believed he would have seen the *exact* same scene that he had from behind the glass. (The thought of what he would be using to see would never have occurred to me as a philosophical problem of infinite regress.)

Trapped in my head

So the visual experiments at first presented me with an uncanny feeling: what if, then, what's out there doesn't correspond to what's in here? What if, for example, what I take to be a pillow is actually a hideous green monster that my perceptual apparatus just translates conveniently as *a soft thing to sleep with? What is that thing over there? I'm trapped in my head!*

But it is this sense of being trapped that is important. It begins to push directly against objectivity: there is no way to verify the sense information we receive. Just like in the story of the little man in my head above, there is no way for me to jump outside my skin and verify objectively that colors, shapes, sounds and other sensory data, are what I take them to be. Furthermore, there is no way for me to even verify that the sense data I am receiving is being caused by the objects I am conditioned to think are causing them. If I am trapped in my head, then so is the whole universe. But this isn't accurate, either, because what I take to be my head is just another object arising in awareness.

Multiplicity resolving into awareness

But is this it? Is this all the direct path wants to take us to, to some radical agnosticism about our perceptions? What would really be the point of that? What is even the point of questioning the existence of separate objects, and what does that have to do with spirituality at all? The old Zen admonition "Don't make one" (because one implies two, three, four, and so on) is instructive here. If one appears, multiplicity (and separation) appears; if one disappears, then so do multiplicity and separation. The experiments in the direct path are going right for the throat of apparent separation: if objectivity dissolves, then so does containment, so do body and mind, self and world, other and self. The house of cards comes down, and all is revealed to be awareness itself.

So, begin to view the world for a moment as if there aren't objects out there. What begins to happen? Oddly, for me one of the first implications of inquiring into objects was its corollary: inquiring into space. Space itself, even visually, is the yin of objects' yang, the nothingness to being, but if objects are truly just color and form, then where is this supposed space that separates me from them? Visually I can't find space. This view collapses the certainty of three-dimensionality, which suggests something surprising: nothing is at a distance from "me." Or, to put it another way, all things are at the same distance. Or, to put it in a way that feels closer to my experience, all visual data is equally intimate.

And this is what the direct path does expertly: it takes a belief, like the belief in objectivity, and it begins to uproot it, methodically, with a clear-cutting logic that—while at first you don't completely appreciate it—becomes clearer and clearer as you go. In some sense, once you begin to grasp the implications of the methodology, it's too late: you can't unsee it! For example, while I haven't fully recognized the truths of the direct path's argument against common sensibles, I intuitively grasp it enough to know that I can't just add a sense for verification, and this has profound implications for how we interpret our experience. It begins to dislodge objectivity, which is really just the first domino in the chain of beliefs that lead to containment, separate self, other, time, space, causality, mind, body, and even truth itself.

Objective truth

And it is on this last point that I wish to comment. I don't know why or how, though this clearly comes out of my reading and conversations with Greg, but the very belief in objective, literal reference itself has come to be deeply doubted. This well-meaning tyrant, which has led me by the nose through countless vocabularies, filling me with an urgency that has been at once as equally thrilling as it has been enslaving.

This is what I was referring to earlier in the piece, in regards to my ever-updating palimpsest. Once objectivity—even in the conventional sense of *things* and *material*—begins to weaken, so also does the idea that there is an objective metaphysics, which exists in some Platonic realm. It's important that we have working vocabularies that help us navigate our experience in the world (we can't avoid this), but we're freed to the extent that we don't take them to be objectively referential.

All paths point to their own dissolution

Once I began to sense this, a huge shift took place in how I approached this path. I began to sense that all the tools were themselves deeply compassionate but, in some way, ultimately empty, too. They would burn up upon use. All paths seem to point to their own dissolution; otherwise, there would be no true freedom. For the first time in my life, the possibility emerged that vocabularies (even those opposing in their claims) might co-exist as useful and helpful.

The epistemic materialist, as well as the physical materialist, wrapped together as they are, also dissolve together.

But I am getting ahead of myself here, ahead of my ice-melting, rock-in-the-shoe self. I have been brought to a special place by the direct path approach, but it is not yet the vista of all-is-awareness. A very powerful tool has been placed in my hands, one that bids me, more than any I've encountered, to look right now at my direct experience. For in it is already the liberation from all teachings.

The Direct Path and Causality
by Priscilla Francis

"I didn't have to disown any of my familial, cultural and religious values and reasoning; likewise the more personalised insights gleaned from key experiences. I still see them as my preferred frames of reference, albeit as tools that do not hold any privileged position over my ongoing intuitions for navigating life. This relaxed outlook gifts me greater clarity for discovering intriguing depths and profound intricacies within those familiar standpoints. I now explore and contemplate them all with even more gratitude and admiration as I find that the wisdom I sought elsewhere was already unceasingly present in my life."

Intimacy and curiosity

Intimacy and joyful ease with life's experiences have always been my heart's most cherished calling. I find that many others, too, share my passion for harmonious living, though in each person the triggers of this zeal, the tools for bringing it about, and the struggles in achieving it seem to manifest themselves in different ways. When I was a child, my curiosity was a great ally in my desire to enjoy effortless ease with my experiences. As I grew older, though, this very questioning nature became a source of discomfort with regard to the events of my life. But serendipitously, this same trait is now allowing me to re-establish a joyful communion with the experiences life presents me.

This is the story of how I started life by celebrating its every moment, and yet came to a point where I felt painfully isolated. To say that growing up distanced me from life would be misleading. The distance was merely my own thoughts about my changing situations. I was never not close to life, and nothing could have caused a real separation. The reversals and shifts in my circumstances were drastic, and I needed to understand why my mind, which had always been considered penetrating and quick-witted, was suddenly failing miserably to adapt fast enough. I puzzled over what was causing me to feel dislocated and estranged in even the most amicable surroundings. My story unfolds to show how I came to understand this seeming loneliness and its causes and effects as mere mirages, by inquiring with the direct path. This story, as most stories, comes along with the paradox created by language. Can I deconstruct causality by telling a story with seeming causes and effects? I will explore this apparent twist in the plot later, when I highlight the openness and joyful freedom underlying the direct-path approach.

Childlike curiosity

When I was a young child, all my little experiences seemed enigmatic to me. Nothing felt ordinary. Everything appeared as a deep and intriguing well of cryptic information waiting to be deciphered. I could spend an inordinate amount of time simply gazing at something. Clouds, the moon, flowers, trinkets, stones, rain drops—I could feel myself bursting with the queries I had about them, but the wonderments were too overwhelming to put into words. I satiated my curiosity by just absorbing as intently as I could with my senses. I enjoyed soaking in the magic of those moments of intimacy—just me and my quizzical scrutiny of events and objects. It felt like enough to simply sink deeper into my mystifying world.

When I grew old enough to construct questions, every appearance and happening seemed like a mystery beckoning me to ask what, where, when, why, and how. From simply observing my experiences in their raw nakedness, I was now starting to build concepts and meanings around them. I pondered over the causes of the different transformations and inconsistencies around me. I wanted to understand the mechanisms and implications of my thinking and emotions. What caused my ideas? How did they get into my head? Why did I remember some things and forget others? Why did some thoughts seem to create specific feelings in my heart? I never grew tired of my questions. They morphed from precise to elaborate, and vice versa, on their own. The answers could never satiate my curiosity, but I didn't expect them to. Instead, they were a delightful launching pad for even more exciting puzzles and queries.

I was equally intrigued by the stories I was told. Stories from the Bible captivated me with their characters and narratives. I wanted to know more about this God who was said to be my loving Father in a place called heaven. More than anything I wanted to know why He was not speaking to me like my parents did. Why the lack of communication? Why the separation from my "Father"? Why did I have to wait until I died to see Him? Why was He not inviting me to visit His home in heaven? My inquisitiveness was starting to lead to dissatisfaction with the doctrines provided by the world.

As I grew older the questions forming around my religious faith multiplied even as my love for God rapidly increased. Why did He severely punish His fallen angels if He was loving and forgiving? I could not imagine a loving person abandoning His own angels for any reason at all. But that question, as well as similarly disturbing ones, was somewhat kept under wraps by the many worldly phenomena that pulled my attention in every other direction. I wanted to investigate the geographical wonders in our world. I wanted to explore its astronomical marvels. I was also absorbed with the rationales for the wide variety of beliefs, rituals, attitudes, values, and lifestyle choices within different communities. There was ample influence of diversity all around me; my school, my neighborhood, and even "exclusive" places like church were interestingly multifaceted because of the cultural plurality of my country. So much to learn about supposed causes and effects!

Curiosity tinged with growing pains

As the years went by, life started to show more of its bittersweet side and the focus of my questioning demeanor changed sharply. My world became disturbingly unfamiliar when my Mum fell seriously ill, and the strangeness increased with her death. My sense of discomfort and bafflement deepened when a similar fate befell my Dad—to the point that I could no longer make sense of the simplest things in life. Why did this happen? What had gone wrong? Where had I missed the signposts? How was I to understand this? I was no longer mesmerized by the variety of life's experiences... just overwhelmed.

Interactions with others became a source of bewilderment, and even everyday tasks seemed like conundrums. I felt weighed down by confusion. I craved to understand what was causing my disillusionment and how my experiences could have deteriorated so radically. I wanted to pin down the exact point at which my life had become unrecognizable. I needed to see what had caused the changes in order to make sense of it all.

Life's element of surprise no longer felt like an exciting adventure to be met with playful anticipation. I loathed the uncertainties that shrouded my experiences. I felt like I was free-falling into a dark and endless chasm—and I longed for a solid set of resonating clarifications that could break my fall.

I trusted causality to provide these answers because it had been ingrained in me since I was young. Safety precautions, the sciences, societal constructs, and religious doctrines—all had their own systems and foundations of reasoning. But the perplexing shifts in my life accentuated my doubts surrounding these well-established conclusions. I still believed that there were answers, but now it seemed that they were somehow hidden from me. I had to find them. My questions were now blazing with an intense urgency. And just as before, the questions had a way of multiplying themselves. They became fertile ground for a whole new level of questioning.

My search for answers

My Catholic upbringing was the only thing that kept me sane throughout these periods of overwhelming grief and confusion. But still I yearned for more. I felt strongly that there was a serene shore calling me home. I was drained and tired, and I longed to swim towards this place of rest. Furthermore, my questions had begun to revolve around the reasons for the existence of life itself, and they were not happy questions. I insisted on knowing why people had to suffer tragedies when we had a powerful God as our caring father. My suppressed questions around my religious beliefs started to resurface insistently. I could not comprehend the exclusivism adopted by much of Christianity. I demanded to know why.

While still mourning the death of my parents, I was invited to try hatha yoga by a kindly meditation guru. Before long I fell in love with the graceful postures executed with focused awareness. That piqued my interest in Eastern methods of meditation and other yogic practices. I chanced upon spiritual teachers from different countries and traditions. I saw the promise of home, the biblical kingdom of God within, in all these different teachings. I was keen to explore and eagerly took them all in like a starving child. My glimpses of the sweet and homey shoreline I had intuited since I was young grew clearer and stronger by the day. And yet I puzzled over why I was being told to learn techniques and fancy cosmologies in order to feel more strongly the presence of a Divinity that was already lovingly available in its omnipresence. Even the ever-increasing spiritual experiences were not fulfilling. Why was life teasing me with sublime occurrences that nourished me and yet left my heart bleeding and aching for even more? My restlessness only grew stronger.

At the same time, I started extending my research to online sources. I came across nondualism on YouTube and Facebook forums. Something in it all resonated deeply, but my questions had by now grown into a gigantic fortress that was a major distraction. My impatience for answers didn't allow me to relax into the truth of the messages I was receiving.

Within weeks from the time I began to scour the internet, one of my Facebook friends introduced me to a gem of a book called *The Direct Path: A User Guide* by Greg Goode.[25] My first significant breakthrough with the direct path came in the area in which I was struggling the most: my acute need for sound, causal explanations. The direct path offers a radical insight on causality: that it cannot be found. This is revealed through meticulous and detailed inquiries into our direct experience of occurrences. I was gently invited to investigate the very thing that was preventing me from being at ease with life. It prompted me to get out of my habitual mode of lazily assuming causal relationships between life's intricate web of events.

The direct path

To show how a direct-path enquiry generally works, let me share one of my disconcerting questions. Perhaps others can relate to it. I have often ruminated over whether I could have avoided unwanted occurrences by making smarter choices, or if a problem could have been solved by engaging it in a better way. I would play out various scenarios in my mind with no practical benefit. I would continue to doubt the suitability of my words and actions. I couldn't simply acknowledge what had passed to be the best I could have managed given the circumstances.

25. See Reading List p.160

Using the direct path, this is how I proceeded to inquire.

First, I inquired into the emotions that led to my need for reasons. I sometimes do wonder about the many inexplicable blessings in my life, but these thoughts don't linger for long, and they only leave me feeling appreciative of life's nurturing surprises. It is the sadder moments that have me asking questions that feel heavy or painful. Looking at my sadness, I wondered what about it was so undesirable. All I felt was an intense or weighty sensation in my chest. The more I observed it quietly, the less unfriendly it appeared. In fact, the apparent innocence of this sensation made me feel restful. It felt like a deepening into a sweetness within. I realized that whatever I said about my "sadness" was just my changing opinions about a mass of sensation in my chest. It was experienced as grief or comfort, depending on the thought that was arising at that moment.

Having seen that my sadness didn't exist in any way apart from the awareness of it, I saw that I had no need to look for the events or actions that could have caused it. But I decided to look for them anyway, just to let this insight sink deeper.

I looked at what immediately preceded the sadness. It was a thought that told a story of a situation. In looking at my direct experience, I couldn't find anything in my thought that could force me to feel a certain way. A thought is nothing more than a sound in my mind. It doesn't refer to anything outside itself. How could it create an emotion or anything at all? There is no creative process perceived in direct experience, and no causal link between the appearance of a feeling and the supposed appearance of the cause of a feeling.

A feeling might follow a thought, but that doesn't mean it is connected to it. It is only another thought that claims that the first thought caused the emotion. Feeling sad because of a noise in my mind simply does not make sense. I put aside my mental inputs to get a clearer picture. Looking at the thought and the emotion as a detached and impartial observer, I realized they were simply unrelated perceptions. Each perception, whether a thought or a feeling, could only point to the awareness of the moment. There was in fact nothing more to the entire drama: awareness was all there was. How could I have insisted on knowing what led to the situation that caused my sadness? The only thing to connect the situation and my emotion was a mere thought. Direct experience revealed nothing objective to hold my questions. They crumbled upon enquiry.

I am looking at my fingers as they furiously tap on the keyboard to express and share my experience with the direct path. Four taps seem to cause the word "four." But is that my direct experience? There is one tap and then an *f* appearing on my screen. And then I see my finger on an *o* on the keyboard. Next, I see *fo* on my screen. Next there is a thought that says, "Well done, Priscilla. You are making progress."

But was I really? Let me have a closer look.

1. Finger on *f*
2. Letter *f* on screen
3. Finger on *o*
4. Letters *fo* on screen

Did each of those appearances cause the next? What is the proof? All I perceived were sensations, which I labeled "my finger touching the keyboard." And then I perceived colours that I called "a black *f* on a white screen." Another sensation, and another black squiggle appeared on the screen, and another thought that said, "I just typed *fo*," and then another thought that said "Yay! I typed half a word."

There is only a succession of perceptions in direct experience: alternating sense perceptions of touch and sight. The perceptions do not touch each other in any way. The thought perceptions come with a story but thought has no way of authenticating the sense perception or constructing a theory about it.

The thought perception, the feeling perception of elation at having completed half a word, and the sense perceptions—all point only to awareness of the moments.

Likewise, there is no possibility for even the most "appropriate" of actions at an earlier moment to have successfully avoided a current mishap. Each action and event points only to the awareness to which it occurs, and it is not able to influence another subsequent action or event. With this insight, I realized that it is baseless to try to analyze the past or predict the future. Analyzing and predicting are usually accompanied by regret, anxiety, and worry. I came to see these as unnecessary burdens.

I also came to see that the assumed "moments," apart from now, are nothing more than another thought called "memory" or "imagination." Memory claims to know a past event. Imagination claims to know an event that has not happened. In direct experience, though, all I ever experience is awareness. Memory and even the concept of time are nothing more than fabrications of thought. And a thought can only point to the very same awareness it seems to be appearing to.

Coming home to open-hearted curiosity

Does this lack of certainty about my day-to-day practical assumptions rattle me? Well, it was a little unsettling at first to know that there is, after all, no objective ground of reasoning to support the theories that seemed to influence my apparent choices. But the liberating benefits far outweigh any initial apprehensions.

I now enjoy a light-hearted dance with what were once urgent and puzzling issues.

I still ask questions, but every time I ask, the childlike wonder of long ago keeps growing in strength. I feel like I am coming home to the innocence and transparency of my existence. I feel more open to being spontaneous, knowing that there are no real missed routes or wrong turns. There are no reasons for the sweet valleys and precarious mountains of life; they are mysteries to be experienced, not solved. There is a sweetness that comes with meeting each moment as a fresh occurrence rather than as a by-product of an earlier moment.

Life continues to present more heart-opening opportunities through my recurring "whys," especially in my interaction with others. I still get hurt when I fail to understand why people act the way they do. Then I remember that there is nothing to understand. Each interaction is a snapshot, a moment that is never going to touch another moment. I actually feel grateful for each exchange, regardless of whether it is hurtful or loving, because its uniqueness is a precious and ephemeral display of life. It's okay for it to remain a question because it is not going to either harm or aggrandize any aspect of my life. It's freeing to release my relationships and communications this way. And I am equally in awe of the many different emotions and thoughts that seem to follow these interchanges. They enrich my experience regardless of how they are labeled. Joy, sweetness, annoyance, impatience, excitement, fastidiousness—I now see them all as beautiful inner manifestations of the pluralistic culture I feel fortunate to belong to.

Another opportunity for openings occurs when I feel pressed to make snap decisions, when there is barely time to think before acting. I used to be displeased with some of these hurried decisions and would get stuck in the mental loop of wondering how I could avoid such careless reactions in the future. I felt compelled to understand all the elements that had contributed to my less-than-perfect responses. But having seen the unreality of causality, I need not be so harsh with myself. If there are obvious and clear lessons, then I learn them. If not, I don't need to over-analyze the episode to try to pry a lesson out of it or feel pressured to create a methodology for avoiding similar mistakes.

I also no longer feel crushed when well-intentioned loved ones remind me of the unfulfilled potentials they see in me. These are merely labels, reinforced by "memory." They do not come with objective reasons. I needn't anguish over what could be causing me to neglect and suppress my "gifts." The only unequivocal gift is the uncaused gift of life itself, treasured in the moment and for the moment. This attitude helps me be even more receptive to the unknown gifts that are alive and inspiring in each fresh moment.

I'm enjoying this new-found ease without having to drop anything that feels important to me. The deconstruction of causality and choice does not in any way translate to their destruction. If anything I now appreciate discernments even more - I can now enjoy cultivating more sensitivity and subtlety for my choices without the rigid structures that limit their full potential. I still explain and justify, when there is a practical need for it, with coherent reasoning and to the best of my ability. I acknowledge the benefits of embracing innovative ideas and noble causes. My heart continues to remember with much gratitude the kindness of many who lovingly reach out to make a difference in my life. I keep all promises that memory says I have made. I don't tell my landlord that the 30 days' worth of rent that is due is just a figment of his imagination. I stay open to better ways to respond to life's appearances. But I don't feel dogmatized by any of it. I am free to relinquish or adopt any mode of interpretation or explanation, in accordance with what feels uplifting and blends well with my own evolving ethics and moral codes.

I didn't have to disown any of my familial, cultural and religious values and reasoning; likewise the more personalised insights gleaned from key experiences. I still see them as my preferred frames of reference, albeit as tools that do not hold any privileged position over my ongoing intuitions for navigating life. This relaxed outlook gifts me greater clarity for discovering intriguing depths and profound intricacies within those familiar standpoints. I now explore and contemplate them all with even more gratitude and admiration as I find that the wisdom I sought elsewhere was already unceasingly present in my life. Each person finds clarity in different ways and sometimes in multiple ways. For me, studying different teachings such as the direct path facilitate more experiential insights. I'm letting my spiritual journey evolve freely and creatively. My love for diversity is encouraging an eclectic mix of approaches that help me feel and enjoy more deeply the reality of the moment.

Going forward, I no longer feel the need for definite outcomes in order to carry on imbibing spiritual teachings. I am inspired to keep exploring simply for the fulfillment that comes from discovery, and the joyful contentment brought on by further insights. I feel the same way about all my endeavors; I don't give undue importance to reasons and am learning to relish each activity for its own sake.

My realization of the illusory nature of causality is helping me to be more flexible, not just with my sense of reasoning, but with all experiences. I can infer that all concepts are open to similar scrutiny that will prove them unfindable. Often my receptiveness to these radical insights is tested, but it is exciting to find new ways to soften my heart and open my mind to more of life. I have found the lost playfulness and fluidity in my inquisitiveness. My infinite adventure with questions is continuing to surprise me as it did when I was a child. I feel like I am back home, even though I never did leave. And this time I know it consciously.

Joyful freedom

Is my story an exact and impartial depiction of my reality? Words can edify and entertain, but do they point to anything real other than my perception of them? My knowing of them is all I can be sure of. And the story they narrate is just a collection of current thoughts. But does that mean I should deprive myself of the gift of words? There is much to be appreciated in language despite its never touching anything beyond itself. The truth and beauty inherent in life is also infused in words.

This brings me to the joyful freedom innate in the direct path, which encourages a generous openness and flexibility towards all aspects of life. This magnanimity extends to freedom from any rigid use of language. Having seen how words are nothing objective beyond thoughts, and ultimately just the knowing of them, I no longer need to see language as a literal and accurate representation of life. I am free to use language metaphorically, and in a manner I deem to be most joyful. My preferred words can be the ones that are most effective, beneficial, compassionate, and humorous, or simply beautiful, elegant, and light-hearted.

As promised, I now come back to the question of the seeming paradox in my story of how the direct path *caused* me to see that *cause* is not operative. With joyful freedom, we are free to adopt a vocabulary that best fits our intentions. It is not about making the words correspond to reality—mere words can never make what they refer to a reality.

In my story there is a series of appearances, like this:

1) Priscilla trusts the concept of causality.

2) Priscilla inquires with the help of the direct path.

3) Priscilla does not believe in intrinsic causality.

However, this is not to say that 2 "caused" 3. A current thought has simply put together a timeline of events for this story. I have adopted a causal language even though I am describing how causality can't be found. This joyful paradox is a freedom that comes from realizing that words do not correspond to what they refer to. Even what the name Priscilla claims to denote, when inquired into, is nowhere to be found. Everything, including a body called Priscilla, is experienced as nothing more than sensations, perceptions, or thoughts. These are never experienced apart from the knowing of them, so I am at liberty to communicate with what I feel to be the most suitable type of vocabulary. I feel free to put my points across without asserting that they strictly conform to any particular "truth" regarding the topic at hand. The direct path does not even expect adherence to its own vocabulary outside enquiry; it liberates me even from itself.

So the question of what is causing my serenity and freedom need not arise for me. I can appreciate the direct path for its beauty without having to measure its benefits. This approach enables me to not give my power away to the teachers and teachings of this world, and yet to honor them for their graceful presence. My contemplations and writings are not held to correspond to a reality beyond what is currently experienced. But I can still appreciate the richness of the reflections that thought seemingly conjures every time I place my fingers on the keyboard. There is nothing other than this here and now. There can be no lack. There is simply an ever present knowing of intimate sweetness pointing back to only itself. I can never not be in the close comforts and familiarity of home—always where I belong.

Postscript

Much has transpired since early 2016 when I wrote this story about my dance with the direct path. I continue to marvel at how each new moment offers a gift of insights I couldn't have imagined.

Deconstructing causality has made me even less reliant on external verification for the heartfelt convictions which I hold lightly yet passionately. I feel no urgency to explore the metaphysical secrets, scientific truths and psychological patterns that claim to reveal the cause of global cruelties and individual sufferings. Though I continue to make informed deductions, they are coupled with a heart that intuits the most benevolent decisions for myself and all. This paradoxical dance between the inner recesses of my psyche and seemingly external stimuli has led me to adopt a vegan lifestyle.

I continue to trust life's mysterious ways, but at the same time I trust feelings evoked by uncertainties, disastrous prospects and the tears of others. Life, to me, is not about indulging a limited persona's fearful projections and erecting a fortress to protect its narrow concerns; but nor is it about ignoring the harsh realities of every living being and the little opportunities to make a difference. I am guided by caution and pragmatism in discerning my choices but circumstantial compulsion to internalise societal conditionings, fear based values and limited perspectives have dissipated. Such impulses to conform and worry do arise but I continue to engage them with a clarity born of deeper insights.

Thus I can welcome the unexpected treasures that come even with so-called anxiety and grief. I celebrate both light and intense feelings with a heart that grows more like the heart of the innocent and inspired child of my herstory. Only this time, the childlike heart is playing with increasingly mature reasonings, interactions, challenges and accountabilities. The dance between mind and spirit appears to have "resumed" but I know the soulful harmony between the two never really ceased.

The spirit of nondual insights gives equal power to my personal intelligence as it does the groundlessness that is the reality of everything. To the extent this is clear to me, the lines between creative choices and sweet surrenders are blurred. There is no contradiction between a river serenely flowing to the pull of the ocean and its clever navigation of the rocks, even as it nourishes the living organisms that flourish in it. It all happens both naturally and intelligently; the blessings of life are diverse and as meaningful as I desire them to be—nothing is excluded.

Now that I have realised that nothing leads to predetermined outcomes, I find a new depth and sharpness to my discernments and ideals. My trust in life is complete and this includes the trust in my own psyche, with a goodwill that is not apart from life and a heart that is happily at ease. To jump with a carefree heart and probe courageously as a spark of truth—knowing that the leaps and dives will be supported by that very same truth; it's the ultimate dance that's allowing me to see the infinite greatness ingrained in life and its diverse expressions.

Release the Releaser
by James N. Hurley

" Turning 72 carries with it all the wear and tear that happens to any machine over time, meaning things start to break down—only now it's so much closer to home. It's my body, not the car or the toaster. I'm smiling inside as I write this, because I suspect some of you who are reading this, if you're from the nonduality camp, might be saying to yourself, "He's still identifying with the body. He's not there yet!" But I have to report that at this stage I can see everything as "me"! And it's not like that's stopped the world from doing what it's doing. "

How it began

This is the story of my pursuit of happiness. I wanted to know what was responsible for the unhappiness and suffering in my life, and how to get rid of it.

Although I'd tried many different approaches, my quest didn't get started in a meaningful way until I learned the Sedona Method,[26] mainly because of the depth of change I experienced by using it.

But when you really get into something, you inevitably discover its shortcomings. That isn't necessarily a bad thing, and in this case, what was missing in the Sedona Method led me to discover what was next, and that turned out to be meeting Francis Lucille and discovering the direct path.

A significant part of my story began when I got into an accident while playing with my best friend and lost my left eye. It was at the onset of puberty, so you can imagine the insecurity and lack of self-confidence my new glass eye caused.

I was not interested in addressing this insecurity through the

---

26. www.sedona.com/home.asp

traditional Western avenues of psychoanalysis and psychiatry. I mean, I already knew the cause of my insecurity. Instead I pursued alternate approaches, a lot of which were Eastern in origin, that seemed more holistic to me and that included experiential aspects as well as analytical.

The sedona method

After several years of working with practitioners of Fritz Perls' Gestalt Therapy, combined with yoga and meditation, and seeking various spiritual teachers as they presented themselves in my search, I was fortunate to meet Lester Levenson.

I experienced something different, something special, in that encounter that really got my attention. As we talked, something about the truth and freedom he spoke of struck me. It was more than just an intellectual conversation. I somehow experienced what he was describing. Being there with him, I could feel a strange calmness. He said he'd discovered something that caused his own suffering to disappear completely. But more importantly, he'd found a peace that was so profound that it was totally satisfying, and it had never left him.

Lester said he could show me what he'd found. His approach was holistic, encompassing body, mind, and spirit, and I wanted that. So I joined him, believing I had found what I'd been looking for all my life: a way to let go of what was blocking me, a way to go free. It was called (and still is) the Sedona Method.

How it worked

I became so good at applying the Method, and it had such an impact on my emotional life, that I became one of his first teachers, traveling the country sharing what I'd learned. The brilliance of the Method was that it showed you how to release emotions on a deep level. What Lester discovered was that our struggles with life's situations that cause us to feel sad, angry, frustrated, anxious, or fearful are due to underlying operating programs—core motivators that are responsible for the creation of our fear, sadness, and anger. These motivators are the basic need for love or approval, the need to control or change things, and the desire for safety and survival. And our emotions are one of the ways we go about trying to satisfy these basic directives.

Here's an example of how it works. A feeling of, let's say, sadness comes up in me. I would trace it back to see what its sponsoring directive was. Was I using the sadness to get love or approval? Was I wanting to control or change something? Was I wanting to feel safe? Once I determined which want was operative, I was presented with a choice, which up until this point I hadn't felt like I had: to continue wanting it or to stop and let it go. Once the source of the feelings was addressed, the feelings would dissipate on their own, as they were no longer needed.

Step one: losing the eye patch

Here's how I applied the Sedona Method to the insecurities caused by my missing eye. When I first met Lester, I was wearing an eye patch. My glass eye tended to cause irritation, so now and then I would remove it and wear a patch. But this time I kept the eye patch on. I told myself that it was because having the prosthetic was too much trouble, but in reality I was still uncomfortable with how it looked. This, mind you, was mainly in my head. Most people just thought I had a lazy eye, no big deal to them.

But on another level the eye patch was a social aid, an attraction of sorts. Women loved it, like I had an Errol Flynn mystique, so it actually worked as a chick magnet. As for the guys, they were kind of intimidated, afraid of the pirate. Ha ha!

Then one day Lester came up to me and said, "Jim, lose the patch. It's hindering your growth." So I took it off, and he was right. All the old feelings—or should I say the remaining feelings—of insecurity showed up on my doorstep.

Step two: losing the insecurities and self-consciousness

The re-occurrence of these feelings was not a problem, because I had the Method, and I was able to let them go, which I did. The Method is unmatched in that area.

It was as easy as meeting someone and making eye contact. Even basic communication between two people involves looking back and forth, from left eye to right eye, stopping arbitrarily on one or the other. When someone's glance quite naturally landed on my artificial eye, it felt as if they weren't communicating with me. I was over here, so to speak, looking back from the seeing eye. When this happened, I would even say to myself, inside, "Over here, over here! I'm over here!" It's laughable now. But then, I experienced the fear of being rejected big-time.

So, applying the Sedona Method, I would see in an instant that I was wanting the approval of the other person. I could let that go! Then I'd see that the encounter made me feel uneasy, uncomfortable, and I didn't like feeling that way. So, the first reaction was resistance to that feeling, because I wanted to change or control it. Could I stop resisting? Sure! Now I could see the uncomfortable feeling for what it was.

Learning to let go of such emotions felt, at that time, like the most power spiritual technique I could find. I mean, I was able to become free right on the spot from most of the limiting feelings or beliefs that arose, even if only momentarily. But hey, the moment-to-moment ability to be free of what I believed then to be negative, unwanted feelings—I'll take it!

But something was missing

But there was something inherent in this path and how I was

74

implementing it that was a problem. It was incomplete. The funny thing is Lester told me so from the beginning. He said I would even have to let go of the Method if I wanted to go "all the way." The Method was intended to help the individual get what they wanted in life, so that they could eventually see that happiness isn't out there in the world but in fact inside themselves.

I didn't actually confront the flaw in the Sedona Method until after I'd met Francis Lucille. But looking back, I remember I noticed it early on, as I was learning the Method from Lester's first and main teacher, Virginia. She was explaining how we perceive: I, through my discriminator, sense what's going on in my environment, and I make decisions on the basis of information I receive. I asked her right after the presentation, "What about the I-sense?" She replied, "That's not important now," and when I asked Lester, he said we could discuss it after I had learned the basic premise of the Method, how to let go. So I set the question aside. Little did I know then that that was the missing component that the direct path and Francis would fully address and clear up later.

Presupposing the me

The Method did work as initially promised—it had life-changing benefits for those who used it—but only up to a point. You most definitely can release feelings. But it failed to address the question of the releaser. Someone believing themselves to be a separate individual can learn the method and use it to remove most of the feelings that arise. Where it failed was that it was incomplete in understanding, and thereby perpetuated the very source of the problem: namely, the idea that we are separate entities who can do something to set ourselves free or otherwise facilitate our own enlightenment.

Using the Method at all presupposed three things: one, that

a me as a separate entity even exists; two, that this me as a separate entity can in fact be free by virtue of something I do or don't do; and three, that life situations and emotions were the problem that needed to be fixed, and by making changes, this me would then be okay!

I was able to see that the very use of the Method supported the idea of a separate individual. Let me give you a real example. I'm in line at an event, and some jerk tries to skip the queue and get ahead of me. My Irish gets triggered, and I want to go to war. But before I approach the guy, I look within at how I'm feeling, and the impulse arises to release the feeling, because it doesn't feel good. This is the Sedona Method.

What nonduality adds

But here's nonduality's contribution: then I stop and ask myself: *who* doesn't like feeling this way? During this introspection there's the unstated understanding that consciousness is always welcoming, whatever is happening, because its very nature is open, empty, and free.

So I choose not to release. Actually, no: I see the activity caused by the me-feeling wanting to get rid of the upset—and I stop there. I'm just witnessing, just being globally open to what's present. And that openness gives room to what's being presented. Not because of something being done, but as a result of the very nature of being this globally witnessing present. Consequently, the sense of me softens, recedes into presence, along with the uncomfortable feelings and the need to say or do anything. After all, this is New York, and people jumping queue is a fact of life here. And so is how other New Yorkers respond. In this case, others online ripped him a new one. Ultimately I didn't have to say a word.

Thus what became so evident was this movement, this movement of wanting to get rid of something, this desire to *do* something, to change what was. Consciousness doesn't do that—a sense of a someone does. This someone, if engaged, only perpetuates the struggle, the wanting things to be different, to continue. The someone was keeping the struggle, and himself, alive.

A lingering sense of separation and fear

I taught the Sedona Method from 1977 to 1993. Lester died in 1994. He was gone now, but I was still troubled by a deep sense of separation and fear. Not suffering, mind you. I was not miserable (at least not yet), but definitely not satisfied. And definitely not at peace.

Lester was the first one to expose me to Ramana Maharshi, Nisargadatta, and nonduality, which I was growing to love. And even though I stopped teaching, I continued to use the Releasing Method in the midst of feeling this lingering dissatisfaction. I continued to seek in a spiritual way, too. My encounter with Advaita through Lester led me to finding out about Robert Adams, Ramesh Balsekar,[27] Papaji (H.W.L. Poonja)[28] and other Advaita teachers, and the love continued to grow.

Francis Lucille

But it wasn't until I first met Francis Lucille and experienced the perfume of nonduality for the first time that things changed. Francis and I became friends. There was a period, over a year and a half, maybe two, in the beginning that I didn't have to work, and I just went to his retreats. I attended lots of satsangs in the NYC area as many new Advaita teachers began to appear on the scene, most notably Gangaji, Wayne Liquorman, and Catherine Ingram. But I just really resonated with Francis.

---

27. Ramesh S. Balsekar (1917-2009), a disciple of Nisargadatta
28. H.W.L. Poonja (c1910-1997), a disciple of Ramana Maharshi

When I first met Francis he invited me to accompany him to his next scheduled meeting, which was in Boston. We drove, which was a wonderful opportunity to just be together in a relaxed way. It was during our ride that I did something that felt egoic, for which I apologized, and Francis immediately said, "Oh don't worry about it, Jimmy. It's not who you are." Imagine knowing you didn't have to kill the ego in order to be free of it!

You see I had grown up believing that the ego, with its wants and desires, was the source of suffering. One could even argue, as the Buddha did, that on an individual level the ego was the problem and had to be gotten rid of. I mean, wasn't it my ego that suffered from being self-conscious and insecure? Wasn't it me who felt jealous when someone I liked showed interest in someone else? Or angry when I wasn't being heard or paid attention to sometimes? After all, didn't the problems somehow have to do with something being wrong with me that I had to fix or overcome? Certain spiritual teachers would even say that in order for there to be enlightenment, the me had to disappear or that thoughts had to stop and the mind had to be quiet. And with the same breath they'd say there was no mind outside of thinking and that the mind was the ego that stood in the way of our true self.

When Francis said to me, "It's not *who* you are," I felt an immediate sense of relief. I felt off the hook, so to speak, because I saw something, a separation of sorts, inside. He then went on to explain that, if I could see the behavior and feeling, if I could stand apart from it, I necessarily wasn't it, and that explained how I was feeling.

Boston was such a wonderful continuation to our first meeting in New York that I wanted to take every opportunity I could to be with him in order to learn everything about the direct path. You see, I was tasting what I had only been reading about all those years concerning the direct path and, for what felt like the first time, I was beginning to know with Francis what those words really meant.

Like when he'd point out that thoughts and feelings happened in the same place as did bodily sensations and sense perceptions, and that "it" was none other than this awareness I referred to as me. *Seeing this was so freeing.* In his company what I'd read became real, became alive.

That in-seeing got my attention, but it was short-lived, as the me-identification with the thoughts, feelings, and bodily sensations was so strong. So I would sit and look at the content of my inner self. I would discriminate, asking myself, *What do I know? What do I see when I look inside?* And it became obvious that thoughts would appear and disappear there inside me. The same held true for feelings, emotions, and bodily sensations. I saw clearly that they were appearing inside me, this awareness. I could not see any difference between me, awareness, and these comings and goings. And then seeing that the perception of, let's say, a chair, or a tree, happened in the same place as my thought or my feeling was mind-blowing. Intellectually it made perfect sense too, that if I as the looker or *awaring* witness, if you will, was that which these thoughts appeared to, lived in, and then disappeared into, they had to owe their existence to this very same awareness.

But that the chair or the tree wasn't outside of me. I don't know...I was having trouble with that one, even though I was experiencing it as such, because it also included, heck, everything, the world. Just goes to show you how strong this idea of a separate me is that I doubted my own experience.

It didn't become really clear that there was no-thing outside until one day while I was reading Atmananda's *Atma Darshan* and *Atma Nirvriti*.[29] Francis Lucille considered Atmananda one of his teachers even though they never met. And I couldn't get enough of reading him, especially this book. It was when I read

29. Both of these works are out of print and not generally available.

the section "The Origin and the Dissolution of the World" for the umpteenth time that something started to percolate. I was struck by his claiming that the truth could be found by tracing the objective world back upstream to its source. I'd wondered what that really meant concerning the knowledge of things that appeared. So I thought, *How do I know the outside world if not through my senses?* I took the sense of touch. I held a pen in my hand and asked, *What's the first thing I know?* And it was clearly that I had a pen in my hand. But I already knew that the word isn't the thing. The word "table" doesn't signify what a table is, does it?

So dropping the words "pen" and "hand," what then did I know? Well, there was the shape and texture I could feel as I moved it around in my hand, but I was thinking again. So what else was present that I knew? Well, I was feeling something, and I had previously done body-work meditations with Francis where he would instruct us to give the bodily sensations room to expand in our awareness. So I did that to what I was feeling in my hand, and pen and hand lost their distinctions. There was just this open awareness of sensations. But wasn't that also something I was yet again naming? Nevertheless, I was seeing what he meant by going upstream, and it was exciting.

So what was further upstream to feeling and sensing? What was present? I knew I was sensing and feeling and, according to Atmananda, it was knowledge that comes to know anything! So there was this knowing of sensations that was present. And as I contemplated this knowing, sensations per se had vanished, and knowledge was all that remained, until I thought, what's upstream from this? Poof! There was nothing! Well, not nothing-nothing—I was just awareness. I repeated that process again and again with the other senses as well. Sight wasn't as clear; I would often get stuck with that one as I would with other things along this path.

Investigating the releaser and discovering awareness

Once I was stuck at an impasse and Francis told me I had to let go of the releaser. "What the hell!" I thought. "What do I do with that? I mean, *I'm* the releaser. How the hell am I supposed to let go of me?" That actually became a seminal moment on my nondual path.

So what to do? Go to the laboratory and begin to investigate. What are the components of what was present?

- ❖ I see there's the awareness of feeling stuck.

- ❖ There's the feeling of not liking being stuck.

- ❖ There's the trying to let it go and a sense of making an effort and being frustrated in the process of failing.

The very first thing I learned in the direct path is to start with the truth, namely that awareness is the subject to which all else, the objects, appear, and that I am that: awareness itself. And as such, awareness is ever present, open, and unmoving. So that's my starting point, I am the very awareness that all I know appears to, and what appears is ever changing. I saw this clearly.

What I saw next was the impulse or movement to try and let go, which also was manifesting as a wanting to get rid of feeling stuck, a desire to change being at an impasse—all of which was an arising in the unmoving awareness that I am. Seeing this was huge. Awareness never moved. As a result, I saw that they were all one and the same arising. There wasn't this multiplicity of things. All of it was how Jimmy was manifesting as this movement.

The releaser sneaks back in

What tripped me up was that the releaser, the separate

me-sense, kind of snuck in the back door as I was trying to do nonduality. The identification with the sense of a separate self can be very subtle at times and can kind of hijack consciousness, if you will. It was actually the same problem I'd had while I was involved with the Sedona Method. I was just seeing it more clearly and deeply.

Awareness is the unchanging, open, unmoving, unfragmented whole that *I am*. What's in the way is the idea that I, as an individual, am trying to let this other idea go, and I can't. The movement was exposed as Jimmy-feeling-frustrated-and-stuck. That was the obstacle. The very movement of the releaser trying to release was exposed. So as the witnessing presence, I just didn't move. Then I saw that there never was this separate Jimmy releaser. It was just an idea arising in me. The problem was seen through and solved, and I didn't have to let it go.

Seeing through the releaser

The in-seeing was the undoing. That was pure Advaita. It also drove home another very important point I'd learned, namely that consciousness isn't a function, a doing. It's always just knowing!

Seeing through the releaser happened many years ago, as I spent long periods of time with Francis. He helped me see that having thoughts and feelings isn't a problem in and of itself; believing that they were real and were who I am is the only difficulty I'd ever had. God, what a relief!

I was on fire back then at his retreats. I mean, imagine being brought face-to-face with the palpable understanding: "You are Zero Distance to all you know!" That little tidbit struck me like a thunder bolt. Years after investigating the ramifications of that insight and understanding, I wrote a (unpublished) book with that as the title: *Zero Distance*.

The on-going path

The need to be around Francis has all but gone. It's been replaced by wanting to spend time with him and other like-minded friends who also like such company. But the looking continues. Actually, it's intensified. Turning 72 carries with it all the wear and tear that happens to any machine over time, meaning things start to break down—only now it's so much closer to home. It's my body, not the car or the toaster. I'm smiling inside as I write this, because I suspect some of you who are reading this, if you're from the nonduality camp, might be saying to yourself, "He's still identifying with the body. He's not there yet!" But I have to report that at this stage I can see everything as *"me"*! And it's not like that's stopped the world from doing what it's doing.

I still experience getting stuck, even... and as I sit with this statement I have to say it isn't really true. The truth is phenomena still arise, and as provocative as they may feel and appear, at no time do I ever feel lost or stuck in or with them, as conscious awareness is ever present, which takes the sufferer out of the picture in the midst of whatever is present living itself out. This is especially so when intense fear arises from some failing body function. Or the announcement by the medical profession that I've got one of those dreaded age-related conditions that could prove fatal. Remember wanting to survive as a body? Well, that feeling is deep—like DNA-deep—and will be as long as I have the slightest identification left with this body.

Reminds me of a story. A Zen master nearing death was asked by a disciple how he was doing. The master replied, "I'm fine, but my body is having trouble keeping up."

So, although I can't imagine not having the wisdom that is available with a nondual-direct-path perspective, and although having this knowledge at the moment brings with it great feelings of gratitude, I can honestly say that the direct path is not a prescription that takes away or otherwise shields one from the vicissitudes of life. In fact, being knowingly the open, non-local field of the present awareness I call James allows everything to be experienced fully.

Even thought. It is crystal-clear here that feelings, bodily sensations, and sense perceptions come and go in this awaring presence and have been recognized as having no power to change either way, positively or negatively, this awareness. I still am confronted with the aches and pains and discomforts of living in a 72-year-old body. And let me tell you it has been intense at times. Because it brings you face-to-face with the inevitable reality that nobody gets out alive. Seeing I am the unchanging reality that the sensations and feelings that comprise this arising body appears to, is the ultimate reward. *And* the reality remains that realizing this arising will, one moment in the time of this life stream, be no more—this sometimes still causes a shudder within. It still exposes yet another layer of a me-identification.

But that's okay! It's part of the whole. Nothing is separate. The me-feeling, the ego-idea, bodily sensation, our assumed humanness—these are all part of the whole, as is feeling free of it all, as is getting stuck in identifying with it all sometimes. The only thing that matters is one's point of view, and sometimes that just takes being willing to be with *what is* unflinchingly until the right perspective shows up, which is, I'm okay no matter what!

An Enquiry into Space
by Kim Lai

"My friend and fellow direct-path student Neil told me something very important: "Inquiry is not about removing the effects of reality by changing experience. It's about removing the false assumptions about knowledge."

Space, the final frontier

Time and Space

Space begets objects and objects beget space. Space must come in to make objects and objects must come in to make space. Therefore, they are both non-existent as such. But it has been proved in other ways also that objects are non-existent. Thus space is an illusion.

—*Notes on Spiritual Discourses from Sri Atmananda,*
Note 121[30]

When I was five years old, I saw *Return of the Jedi (Star Wars: Episode VI)* in the cinema. The film made a very strong impression on me. This cinema session became the cornerstone of several strong interests that are still with me today. One of them is science fiction; after *Star Wars*, I watched *Star Trek* and other sci-fi films and shows in my childhood, and I started reading sci-fi novels as a teenager. Later, *2001: A Space Odyssey* marked me for life. I love the whole film, but my favourite part is a scene in which a spaceship gracefully drifts in emptiness, and then slowly docks on a space station orbiting around earth. The slow pace emphasizes the immensity of space.

30. See Reading List p.160

I am attracted to large empty places. Open ocean horizons, mountain tops, and huge warehouses such as the Tate Modern Museum's Turbine Hall in London make me feel calm, open, available. I probably share this attraction to wide and open space with most people. As much as we love other people, most of us—and particularly city-dwellers like me—feel the need to go to places where the distance between us and surrounding objects or people is as great as possible. We seek large open spaces, and perhaps even space-travel stories, for their peace. They seem to have a calming and regenerative power.

Despite my interest in science fiction and my attraction to empty places, before I became interested in nonduality, and later more specifically in the direct path, I rarely—if ever—thought of space. I just took it for granted. I tacitly accepted the general view of our culture that the three dimensions of space (and time, which could be considered its fourth) are the background of the universe; all galaxies, solar systems, planets, stars, living organisms, or specks of dust exist in space, which has to be there first to support the concrete matter they are made of. Like most of us, I would have concurred with the *Oxford Dictionary*'s definition of space as "the dimension of height, depth and width within which all things exist and move." Indeed, this definition is aligned with the basic assumptions of our culture: space and time preexist, and objects made of matter exist within them. Without space, matter could not exist. It would literally have nowhere to stand, no volume to take its three-dimensional shape. We cannot even think of the absence of space. It makes no representational sense.

Everything in its right place

Just as I had not yet started to question space, I was not thinking about awareness very much. Like space, awareness seems like an *a priori* given: without even needing to formulate it, I operated under the assumption that each human being is an object made of organic matter, including a brain, which generates an awareness—I didn't know how—which, I believed along with everyone else around me, is personal and unique. Thus awareness and body are considered inseparable: the former is supposed to be a by-product of the latter. I felt that my individual essence—my core, what I really am—was somewhere behind my eyes, in my brain. In this framework, I had no other choice than to implicitly assume I was an independent awareness, enclosed in a body made of matter and occupying space: located at a particular position, with an open view on a pre-existing world. The two assumptions that space exists and that I am located in space feed each other.

How does it feel to occupy a position in space? Well, it feels like my entire experience is happening in space and is informed by spatial relationships. First, I experience space through my senses. I see a world of objects spreading out in space. Colours, sounds, smells, or textures inform me how close or far from me objects are. Additionally, the movements of objects and of my body create changes in perception, such as modifications of the colours I see, which reinforce the sense that materiality is a fact, an unchallengeable given.

Second, I experience my body as an object in space, through my five senses. I can also feel my body and locate the feelings: my head, my chest, and my toes feel like different places. Moreover, I know in which position various parts of my body are. I feel my body's volume and position in space.

Third, my mind and its content seem inextricably linked with location and spatiality. Although they are not material per se, I feel like my thoughts happen in a particular place, generally in the front part of my brain. Besides, when I think of an orange, I see it in three dimensions: in my mind's eye it shows up in space.

Furthermore, perceptions are often accompanied or followed by a thought. If I hear a car passing in the street while my
eyes are closed, I see a thought-image of a car, which reinforces
my knowledge that the sound was produced by an actual car.

Finally, I feel like my awareness is personal and works like
a container; objects can be inside or outside of it. If I stand in
front of my house, I can see it, because it is inside my awareness.
But when I am at work, I cannot see my house anymore, because
it is now outside the reach of my awareness. As a point in space,
I have access to a limited number of the things made of matter
that space contains. Other things that are out of reach still seem
to exist, even if their existence cannot be verified through the
senses at this very moment.

Questioning the notion of space

A few years ago, I became interested in nonduality, and this
interest led me to challenge the materialist views of my culture. I went to many meetings and read many books. Space
and time were a recurrent topic in the meetings I attended and
in the dialogues I read. I heard and read phrases like "there is
no time," "space is only an illusion," "boundlessness is all there
is," and "everything appears in consciousness, including space
and time." I became fascinated by these ideas. I explored various approaches, and then discovered the work of Jean Klein,
Francis Lucille, Rupert Spira, and Greg Goode. I fell in love
with the direct path and delved into it: I read Nitya Tripta's
Notes on Spiritual Discourses of Shri Atmananda[31] and used the
experiments in *The Direct Path: A User Guide.*[32]

Direct-path enquiry uses sublation, a process that lets the
student realize that every object of the world (like an orange or

31. See Reading List p.160
32. See Reading List p.160

a rock), of the body (like my arm or a feeling in my chest), and of the mind (like thoughts, moods, choices) are nothing but awareness. For example, Experiment 2, "Seeing the Orange," is intended to show how a simple object like an orange is in fact never experienced objectively, and is nothing more than aware- ness. After repeating the experiment a few times, I was struck by this very simple point: space is never experienced directly. It is mentioned right at the beginning of the book and does not require a nondual understanding or even the use of sublation. Whether I look at a wall, at the sky, at a computer screen, or at a mountain in the distance, I do not see any space, simply—and quite amazingly—because I *cannot* see space. All I—and any other life forms equipped with eyes—can see is expanses of colour. As Sri Atmananda puts it in *Note 469*:

> Do you perceive space? If so, with what organ? If you say "with the eye organ," it can perceive only form. Space is not form.

How mind-blowing to realize that space, the basic premise of material reality, is in fact never perceived directly. I was amazed.

Investigating from the wrong place

I kept inquiring into objectivity and space, with honesty and earnestness, the two qualities Atmananda deems necessary for direct-path students. I was interested and motivated, but I failed to realize my most basic mistake: I was bringing expectations into my enquiry, because I lacked clarity on my motivations. In a fascinating group discussion, Greg pointed out that there are two main motives for nondual enquiry. At first, a person might want to reduce, or even eradicate, his or her suffering, and reach a state of bliss, or in other words, *be enlightened*. This motive—let's call it motive A—is often the one that draws students to the direct path. It gives momentum to the search, but the expectations it creates soon become counterproductive, because it's still about acquiring something personal. The second motive—motive B—is to lift the veil of illusion, to know the truth. It stems from a sincere curiosity, and it is free from end-gaining and attainment objectives.

In my case, motive A was dominating. I had an idea of where the enquiry into objectivity and space was supposed to take me. I expected a shift in perception. My expectation was based on things I had heard in nonduality meetings, and things I had imagined: although they question the existence of space and material reality in general, nondual teachings use spatial metaphors too, in an attempt to express an inexpressible absence of limitation. Words such as vastness, openness, and boundlessness are favourites. On the one hand, it seems paradoxical and counterproductive to use the very notions you are trying to debunk as tools in your demonstration; on the other hand, the impossibility of avoiding spatial metaphors, even for the most hardcore materiality-denying Advaitists, shows how deeply spatial notions are embedded in our language. Besides, banning spatial metaphors from one's vocabulary would only result in creating an affected, pretentious language. It would be as futile as the infamous tendency to speak without using personal pronouns that strikes some nondualists.

My enquiry into objectivity was flawed because, contrary to my belief, it was not honest. I did not know exactly *what*, but I expected *something* to happen. I was sure that the irremediable impact of this expected, yet mysterious, change would be a proof that enquiry had done its job. Because nondual teachings were saying that space did not exist, I thought that even the illusion of space had to make way for…something else. In that sense, I was awaiting a change in the perceptual experience of vision: perhaps, for example, perspectives were going to flatten, or colours would glow in a new and permanent way.

Discussions with friends in an online group focused on the direct path helped me to realize that making a shift in perception the condition for considering my enquiry successful was counterproductive, for two reasons.

First, we discussed the difference and implications of motives A and B several times, and I got some clarity on the difference between the two motives, and on my own intentions, from those conversations. I realized that expecting my experience of space would change was an expression of motive A. Besides, this process made me realize that meta-enquiry[33] is important, even if one is earnest. Collective critique and self-critique may allow a student to uncover assumptions, flaws, and weaknesses in his or her enquiry, and to refocus in order to allow the enquiry to be more fruitful.

Second, my friend and fellow direct-path student, Neil, told me something very important: My friend and fellow direct-path student Neil told me something very important: "Inquiry is not about removing the effects of reality changing experience. It's about removing the false assumptions about knowledge." Although I had heard statements like this one many times, and although I thought I knew that only the belief in *maya*—and not the illusion itself—needs to be seen through, Neil's statement hit home, and I started seeing my enquiry into objectivity and space in a new light.

Where am I, and where does everything appear?

In the direct-path inquiries on objectivity, we first look for an

---

33. 'Meta (from the Greek preposition and prefix meta—μετά— meaning 'after', or 'beyond') is a prefix used in English to indicate a concept which is an abstraction behind another concept, used to complete or add to the latter.' Thus a meta-enquiry is the process of reflecting on one's enquiry to ensure that one is on track.

object that is performing perception. We try to establish if there is any arising that is doing the seeing (or hearing, touching, tasting, smelling), and we fail to find one. My enquiry into space helped me to realize that there was something really subtle that was not to be missed here. Even though I could not find a colour that was the seer, I was assuming that the *sensation* behind my eyes was doing the seeing. So even if I could not find an object that was causing and resembling the perception, I was still associating the witness with a perceptual object (a bodily sensation). This feeling of being located in a sensation logically implied a separation and even a distance between me-as-a-sensation and other arisings, and this distance had to be in some sort of space.

Once again, I discussed the matter with fellow direct-path students, and the discussion confirmed my intuition that this feeling—that I was a sensation located in the skull—had to be investigated on its own, as part of an investigation into the body. I was able to set this issue aside and resume my enquiry into objectivity. Locating myself in a sensation in the skull had been derailing that enquiry. The point of the first step of the "world" inquiries—when I looked for me-as-an-object—was that I could find neither a perceiver appearing *in* or *as* an arising, nor an objective orange that was causing and resembling the orange-coloured patch.

As this became clearer, I was now able to focus on the next stage of the enquiry and investigate the colour-arising and specifically the notion of its presence and its absence. At this stage, I felt like the colour was appearing in some kind of space. In other words, the core assumption of objectivity was operating: it seemed to me that a colour could exist outside of seeing. If that was true, the colour had to be *somewhere else* when it was outside of awareness, in *some sort of space*. Granted, an independent orange-coloured patch is subtler than an independent orange made of matter that causes the orange patch, but it is based on the same assumptions. So I tackled the problem of space directly. I used the enquiry up to the point where I could see that there is no object that causes or resembles the perceptions; but instead of directly moving to the next step (looking for a difference between colours and seeing), I added a stage: I looked for a space in which the colours were arising.

Let me explain. In an everyday sense, when I put two oranges on a table, I can verify that there is an empty space between them. But when I looked at the same setting while considering only colour arisings, rather than "oranges," I could not find any space either *between* colours or *behind* them. Although space is verified *thanks to* colours (they come first and provide the reference points that allow the three dimensions of space to arise), the opposite is not true: colours as perceived arisings do not need space to arise. In other words, space needs colours to exist. Colours need seeing to arise. And, I assumed, seeing needs a space to arise. But upon examination, this last assumption turned out to be false. When I looked at experience through the direct-path lens, it was much simpler: I found that the succession of colours is continuous, uniform, and infinite. There is no edge, no limit, and certainly no space. This is what "seeing" means in this case: colour arises, without any relationship to a perceiver, to a seeing apparatus, or to a seeing modality, none of which are ever found.

Space opening to somewhere else

Just as they hindered my enquiry into the world, my assumptions about space had consequences for my enquiry into other aspects of experience. Deconstructing objectivity is often the hardest part of this enquiry, and in most cases, once a student has really seen through objectivity, the rest seems easier. I realized for myself that the rest is definitely harder if objectivity has not been deconstructed.

This became particularly obvious when doing direct-path experiments about containment. Their purpose is to check if awareness acts like a container, if it is contained by anything, if it has limits we can establish. I felt drawn to these experiments and did them many times, but without realizing that I was still assuming space was the framework of arisings. During the experiment, I was checking arisings with a kind of invisible hand, to see if they marked a limit; before gaining some clarity about space and objectivity, I did not realize this way of looking assumed that arisings were tangible and within a space, which made the enquiry unfruitful. Indeed, the success of this experiment relies on having seen through objectivity, and most importantly, the three main parts of the direct-path enquiry—world, body and mind—are in that order intentionally. Additionally, the most basic steps of an experiment, particularly the simplest experiments on materiality, may require a lot of practice and genuine interest—some motive B—to be fruitful.

Before learning this lesson, I was going through the entire book *The Direct Path: A User Guide*[34] and doing each of its 40 experiments once. To some extent, this technique gave me a taste for the path, a good overview, and even a few insights. But the revelations it brought about, although they seemed deep at the time, were short-lived. This became more and more obvious: deconstructing physicality is paramount; the experiments on the world comes first in the book for a reason. Although I had been warned from the start, I had to find that out for myself, through enquiry and through discussions with fellow students.

As this issue of space settled and stopped bothering me so much, I came to understand that it is not considered very important by teachers, simply because it is only an aspect of objectivity. The real problem I face as a student is not to understand why or how space is an illusion; the main issue is to understand why a "seen" colour makes no sense.

34. See Reading List p.160

Assuming that we see a colour implies that a colour is in place, able to be seen and unseen. If a colour can be unseen, then awareness is limited and has parts; it has an inside and an outside, and arisings can be in it and out of it. I sometimes feel like awareness is like a website, with a front end and a back end. Any website has both: the pages that we see when we visit the site are the front end, and the content on those pages and their design is controlled through a back end, another set of web pages that the site visitor does not see but that lets the site administrator control the site. Although the back end is not visible, it exists, and there could be no front end without it. In other words, the back end is present somewhere else, in another location, hidden from us, but real.

This potential back end is nothing more than the basic principle of objectivity, the possibility that an arising can exist outside of consciousness. Inquiring into space, I discovered, had been for me an entry point to this main issue: does an unthought thought make sense?

When Two and Two Are Really One
by David Boulter

"I can quite happily interact with my friends and family, my community, my colleagues, and my career without having to get all nondual and say that none of it is real.... I can entertain all manner of thoughts without having to believe that what they say is ultimately true. I am also free to use thought as a tool in my everyday life without having to try to silence my mind with the attitude that because thoughts are neither true nor false in direct experience then they are useless in practical contexts and should be shunned."

Stuck in my head

It was a bright Saturday afternoon, the park full of the sounds of families making the most of the early spring sunshine. But I was oblivious to all this. I was sitting at a picnic table, scraps of paper and bits of twig laid out in front of me, lost in an endeavour to find out whether there was any evidence for the assumption that two plus two did, in fact, equal four.

It's a good thing none of my students could see me. I'm a mathematics teacher with a couple of decades' worth of experience. Was this a sign that it was finally time for me to quit the chalk-face and spend more time with the begonias? Or was there something else going on here? Let me explain.

It is said in the direct path that when you stand as a body, you experience bodies; when you stand as mind, you experience minds; and when you stand as awareness, awareness is your experience. I've always been a mind kind of a guy.

Since I can remember I've had a thirst for discovering how the universe ticks and is put together. Even as a child I was aware of the ultimate questions of existence and needed to know more.

This desire led to an interest in the physical sciences. I loved science at school but was never really interested in the practical aspect. It was the theory that was my passion—how does this work? How does that happen? Why this way and not that?

This love of science eventually led me to studying the sciences at university, and, initially at least, to a career in a lab coat. As far as I was concerned, science held all the answers, opening up whole new quantum worlds that at first looked to be the key to the questions I was asking. But although I kept looking, science never seemed to cure the itch. As more questions were answered, all that happened was that new questions were raised. I learned an awful lot, but in the end I realized that science was never going to lead me to the ultimate answers I was seeking. The search was leading to frustration, keeping me stuck in my head. I realized that there had to be a way forward.

That way forward soon took a more esoteric turn.

The spiritual marketplace

I had been raised as a Roman Catholic, and at one stage had been active in the Church. And while it never seemed to provide any of the answers I was looking for, it did instill in me a love of all things spiritual. So in my quest I went the way travelled by many seekers and discovered the new-age spiritual marketplace. Tarot, reiki, brainwave entrainment, *I Ching*, lucid dreaming— you name it, I dabbled. What was even better at that time was that there was this new-fangled craze called the internet that was becoming increasingly popular. My metaphorical prayers were answered. I could now endlessly search for a myriad of books and articles, all of which would answer my questions on life, the universe, and everything.

Only they didn't.

It seemed that all I was being asked to do was to believe in a whole new set of facts. With so much material available to explore, I'd spend a month or two on one thing before moving onto the next—bored with the Kabbalah? How about Celtic shamanism?—and what was more frustrating was that many of the so-called ultimate truths you'd be given by one book totally contradicted the so-called ultimate truths in another. What was the consumerist seeker to believe? Then there was that other phenomenon I didn't know existed until this point: pseudoscience. This is the art of dressing spurious facts in respectable clothing, but in reality it is little more than a snake-oil salesman in a lab coat. Most of what I read simply withered under examination.

After several years of this I was getting jaded and was at belief overload. By this time I was in deep, having spent the previous seven years in a fraternal brotherhood. And while dressing up in robes and banging gongs is great fun (don't ask) I still wasn't getting close to the answers that I'd been seeking all this time. The questions were being answered, of course; it's just that these answers didn't seem at all satisfying. So if science wasn't providing me with what I needed to know, but then neither was the spiritual marketplace nor the faith of my upbringing, what was a boy to do? (Or in my case, a man in his forties. But you get the gist.)

It was then that in my regular searching of the internet I came across the direct path.

The direct path: seeing beyond the questions

I had come across nonduality before—everyone read *The Power of Now*[35] at the turn of the millennium—but this was different. Yes, there were experiments to follow, which appealed to the inner scientist in me, and yes, there was an online community where you could connect with fellow direct-path students. But there was more than that. The direct path looked to be a way out of seeking, a way that wasn't about having questions

35. Tolle, E. (2001) *The Power of Now*, Yellow Kite

answered, but about seeing beyond the questions in the first place. Because what the direct path seemed to be saying was that I had the whole thing backwards. Where I'd been looking to find answers to an unlimited number of questions, what I really needed to be exploring was the nature of the questions themselves; whether I could find the mind that asked the questions; and whether there was even a questioner to start with.

I was hooked.

One thing I hadn't realized at the time, but later came to discover through nondual enquiry, was that science and mathematics don't actually describe anything "out there" called reality. What they do is to model it. An equation that describes the motion of a ball in the air, or an explanation of the workings of the eye, is really a generalized description. What I had been trying to do all this time was to find a conceptual map that most accurately modeled what was going on with the world because this was what I'd assumed conceptual models were supposed to do. But what I was about to attempt was to question whether it was even possible for thought to do such a thing. Can thought accurately mirror reality?

This was how I found myself sitting at a picnic table that spring Saturday afternoon, busy trying to discover whether there is any objective truth in the statement that 2+2=4.

Investigating an abstract (mathematical) thought

The target of my exploration was a purely abstract thought. Now, of course, within the realm of mathematics, 2+2=4 is about as basic as it gets. This equation is almost as basic as simple counting. But my exploration was doing a little more than just accepting the arithmetic. It was using this arithmetic as an example of a more general question: does a conceptual thought actually mirror anything outside of awareness? Does anything "inside" awareness accurately match something "outside" awareness? Is there even an inside and an outside to awareness? Is there any evidence in direct experience of the kind of mirroring we believe takes place? And if there isn't any evidence in the case of something as basic as 2+2=4, then what about other conceptual thoughts? Then why would we need to believe in this mirroring? I was pretty sure that I wouldn't need to examine every notion, concept by concept. No, the enquiry was designed to pull the plug on *all* concepts. And by liberating me from concepts this would free me from the perpetual need to find any kind of answer or explanation.

What I had to do now was roll up my sleeves and get down to business. So what did I discover?

I first approached the problem as if I were teaching a young child the basics of arithmetic. On my pad I wrote down the equation "2+2=4." This, of course, proved nothing. It was just taking a thought and presenting it in a different, albeit more concrete, way. Breaking the problem down into what seemed like its constituent parts looked to be the way to progress, so the next step was to write "1+1+1+1=4," which wasn't really any better. Neither was writing down "1+1=2, so therefore 2+2 must equal 4." The issue was that I was still referring to abstract thought. There was a feeling that the statements I was writing down were true, but outside of this sensation of rightness nothing was really being proven. A different approach was needed. I needed to get even more basic.

Trying to move from thought to reality

There is archaeological evidence to show that counting goes back at least fifty thousand years. It was originally developed to keep track of animals, tribe members, and property. The first method used was, not surprisingly, to count using the fingers. This is, of course, the first method young children use today when they first meet the concept of counting and basic number work. This method of counting later developed into the use of tallies, which were made by carving notches onto pieces of wood, bone, and clay. The number "one" we use today is in effect a tally mark made originally by pressing the fingernail into soft clay, a mark that has survived for forty millennia.

I was outdoors in the countryside, so there was no shortage of twigs, pebbles, stalks, and other natural objects I could use to represent the numbers I was trying to add together. I grabbed a collection and set to work. I placed these objects on the ground and on the picnic table, in pairs, in singles, as a four, but no matter how I arranged them I was no closer to proving that two add two equals four. Using objects was just like writing things down, but in a more tactile way. The feeling still persisted that the equation was true, but a feeling isn't really good enough. Sure, every time I laid down stones or twigs in two pairs, thought said there were four in total, but I was never getting out of the realm of thought. Something was missing.

Many will remember the 1980s BBC television comedy *Blackadder,* staring Rowan Atkinson as the title character, and Tony Robinson as Baldrick, his hapless servant. At the beginning of one episode Blackadder tries to teach Baldrick the basics of arithmetic.[36]

"If I have two beans and then I add two more beans," asks Blackadder, "what do I have?"

"Some beans," comes the reply.

"Yes...and no. Let's try again, shall we? I have two beans, then I add two more beans. What does that make?"

"A very small casserole."

I was beginning to feel a bit like Baldrick. But why? What was the difficulty with such seemingly simple mathematics?

Anyone who has followed the direct-path experiments will have probably sat with an orange in order to discover what they

---

36. *Blackadder II*, episode 2, "Head," BBC TV, January 1986

really see when confronted with a physical object. What is usually found as a result of the enquiry is that no objective orange is found to exist outside of the colour orange, and that there is no experience of an independent orange anywhere that is somehow causing this colour to appear. Then when this colour is looked into it is realized that colour is never experienced independently of seeing. It's not that colour is out there somewhere, unseen, waiting in the wings to make an appearance, but that colour and seeing are the exact same thing. You can't have one without the other. The enquiry into vision then comes to the conclusion that we cannot experience seeing to be independent of witnessing awareness. Again, there is no vision anywhere "out there" that gets picked up by awareness. And it isn't that there is awareness of colour. There is no seer/seen duality experienced in any way.

Not finding the object—no orange, no number

By progressing in this way it is therefore seen that visually the orange is nothing but colour, which is nothing but seeing, which is nothing but witnessing awareness. Following this discovery, the direct-path experiments go on to look at the other senses in detail, but the same thing is discovered with these too, that no orange is found to exist independently of sight, hearing, smell, touch, and taste, none of which are other than awareness. This is certainly one in the eye for the claims of realism, namely that external objects cause mental objects and that mental objects represent and resemble external objects.[37] There is freedom in this realization as it dispels the notion that there is separation between you on one side and a world on the other. You no longer have to think in terms of being adrift in a world of objects. Once it is seen that no objective orange is ever discovered in direct experience, no matter how hard you stare at it, bang it, smell it, touch it, or bite into it, then it makes absolutely no

---

37. See Reading List p.160: *The Direct Path: A User Guide*, p. 35.

sense to say that there is an orange set there in front of me. The thought "There is an orange on the table in front of me" makes no sense. It refers to nothing independent of awareness.

This was the issue I was facing with my twigs. I was using them to represent numbers, but outside of thought, these twigs were nothing but sensation. They were colour and texture (and had there not been so many dogs around, I could have even tested them for smell and taste, too!). And sensation is nothing but witnessing awareness; it certainly doesn't represent anything concrete. Any idea that these twigs represented any kind of external truth about the objectivity of arithmetic simply wasn't evident. Looking in this way there wasn't even any evidence that there were twigs in front of me, let alone anything they could represent.

The same issue arose no matter how the situation was modelled. So even if I reverted to pen and paper, the marks on the page were still experienced as nothing but colour, which is nothing but vision, which again is nothing but witnessing awareness. The figures weren't experienced as a series of blue marks standing out against the white of their background; the experience was one of unbroken awareness. There wasn't one, two, or four of anything. No matter what I used to do the counting everything arose and disappeared into witnessing awareness in the same way as the orange had. Even though it feels like the content of thought should mirror something outside of thought, that simply wasn't the experience.

It was at that point that I threw the twigs in the air and went for an ice cream.

Thoughts are neither true nor false

So did this mean that the opposite was true, that 2+2 doesn't equal 4? Well, no. Just because the idea that 2+2=4 cannot be verified in direct experience doesn't mean that the opposite is therefore the true state of affairs, either, that 2+2 doesn't equal 4. It isn't that the original thought wasn't being accurately mirrored and that its opposite is a more accurate reflection of what is going on. The point is that there is no mirroring going on at all. Notice that the words "mirroring" and "reflection" are physical metaphors. Mirroring is the idea that an object can be held up to a mirror and that the object and its reflection can be compared for their similarities. This isn't what's going on here. The enquiry shows that the idea of mirroring is not supported by direct investigation and makes no sense as an assumption about our experience. There is simply no mirroring experienced either way, true or false.

And this is also why the enquiry pulls the rug from under any other conceptual thought. The investigation showed that the only connection between the thought "four" and four sticks on the ground in front of me was another thought that claimed this was the case. Indeed, the whole idea of connection is itself only a thought. And as it's not just twigs that are found to be nothing other than witnessing awareness—following the direct path's investigations it can be seen clearly that the whole of the physical world arises as sensation—then there is nothing "out there" for *any* concept to mirror. They all fail in the same way as 2+2=4 does.

Thoughts are inseparable from awareness

The realization even goes deeper than that. Just as the twigs and the marks on the paper are seen to be nothing other than witnessing awareness, the same can be said of the actual thought claiming that 2+2=4 as well. Thoughts are known. It doesn't make any sense to consider there being a thought that isn't. And being known means they are inseparable from the awareness out of which they arise. Awareness is their reality. Thoughts are neither true nor false, but instead can be said to be made from truth.

I've had many other insights through carrying out the direct-path experiments, but that Saturday afternoon enquiry into conceptual thought was a big one for me. As I said at the beginning of this chapter, I've always been a mind-centric kind of guy. To discover that conceptual thinking isn't mirroring anything objective was huge. The effect in the short term was to quieten thought down considerably. Over the longer term, thinking returned, but in a lighter way. It didn't have to be entertained as much. Thinking became a tool rather than the centre of my identity. I am not my thoughts.

There were further implications, of course. I have a career as a teacher of mathematics. How could I go back to school the following Monday and teach my students something I'd discovered had no basis in objective fact? I'll tell you how: like I'd always done, that's how.

It would have been easy at that point to go on and say that I'd seen through mathematics, that ultimately the whole field was a lie. That it was a house built on sand and I wanted nothing more to do with it. But to say all of that would have been a huge mistake and a mixing of levels. It would, in effect, have been giving credence to the thought that mathematics isn't true. A statement that is nothing more than a brand new abstract concept. I hadn't come this far to be tripped up by fresh beliefs masquerading as nondual truths. That thought arises out of and dissolves back into awareness just like any other. I am as free of that statement as I am about thoughts of oranges and arithmetic. The freedom that results from carrying out these inquiries leads to liberation from any such belief.

Suspending disbelief

Downstairs from me at school is the English department, where they teach a lot of Shakespeare. If you watch or study the works of the Bard you don't have to assume that Romeo and Juliet have their own reality outside of the play in order to enjoy the drama. You can get involved in the story without having to believe any of it is true. There is a willing suspension of disbelief. For me it is exactly the same with mathematics.

I am just as free to teach mathematics now as I was before, but with perhaps a touch more lightness. There is no need to treat mathematics as something inherently true that stands apart from who I am. It isn't that there is some monolithic entity called mathematics that exists over there while little old me remains over here, the two coming together periodically in order to exasperate teenage students. It's more the case that teaching situations, squiggly equations on the whiteboard, complex questions, and thoughts about numbers arise out of awareness and dissolve back to where they came from. It isn't that I even need to treat any of these arisings as self-contained objects. They certainly aren't separate from who I am.

The implications for this far exceed mathematics, of course. If no thought ever refers to anything objective then there is never a need to take any thought seriously. This includes all of our beliefs, which are really nothing but thoughts and attitudes taken about other thoughts. Beliefs are just concepts. So if no thought can be verified in direct experience, then no belief can be verified either.

Most of us live lives that are shaped by our attitudes to the beliefs we hold. Think of some of the many beliefs we entertain in our daily lives each and every day:

- *My team is the best.*
- *There is a god who causes good and bad things to happen.*
- *What goes around comes around.*
- *Coffee is bad for you.*
- *I'm not worthy.*
- *She is ugly.*
- *I am fat.*

- *When you die you are dead, nothing more than that.*
- *Winter is coming.*
- *I'll never get a tune out of this violin.*
- *That bit when he said he went for an ice cream didn't really add anything to the narrative, did it?*
- *These people are taking our jobs.*

Many of the beliefs we hold are fairly neutral, but many can be a source of conflict or suffering, often on a global scale. If my beliefs lead me to think I can persecute other members of society or that I am in some way not good enough, then something is perhaps not quite right. This is where the direct-path enquiry on concepts can also help.

Remember, the point isn't to say that thoughts aren't true. If that was the case then that would mean that the opposite to any belief could be the real truth instead. I could rewrite the list above with the opposite viewpoint and they would still be a set of beliefs with the potential for causing conflict or suffering. No, the point being made here is that a belief makes a claim that it somehow mirrors some situation or state of affairs that exists objectively somewhere "out there." As this enquiry into thought, both concrete and abstract, shows, this is never the experience.

Seeing through beliefs

So perhaps I believe that I am a danger to other vehicles when I drive my car. By inquiring into each part of that particular belief—the existence of something I call "my car," the me that drives the car, the concept of danger, the objectivity of other vehicles, the question of "when" something happens—I can start to see through such a belief. And when the objectivity of each aspect of the belief is realized to be nothing more than witnessing awareness, then it can be seen that it isn't that my belief was wide of the mark, but that there was never any mark in the first place. It isn't that the belief contains elements of truth, or that the truth depends on context, or that I need to put a positive spin on what is being told and fix a wide grin to my face. Nondual enquiry isn't about self-help and positive thinking; it's far more powerful and liberating than that. It is seeing that the belief isn't mirrored in any way in the world "out there" and it is allowed to collapse into awareness. No true or false position needs to be taken.

I can quite happily interact with my friends and family, my community, my colleagues, and my career without having to get all nondual and say that none of it is real so I don't have to bother or care. I can entertain all manner of thoughts without having to believe that what they say is ultimately true. I am also free to use thought as a tool in my everyday life without having to try to silence my mind with the attitude that because thoughts are neither true nor false in direct experience then they are useless in practical contexts and should be shunned. That would be just another example of nondual dogma gone wrong. It would also be another pesky concept.

Back in the park I'd reached a point where I could bring my enquiry to completion. It was as if a weight had been lifted. All around me Saturday afternoon life went on. For me nothing had really changed, but in a way it felt like everything had. I felt a kind of relief and a great deal more spacious. It was as if thoughts and beliefs were passing through me, visiting rather than sticking around. I experimented with a few beliefs that I seemed to have been carrying around with me for many years—I believe that I am a teacher, I'm not great at parallel parking, I'm quite good at the guitar but if I practised more then I would be a hell of a lot better. All of these beliefs seemed to float away. They ceased to have any kind of power.

With this new-found lightness I packed up my things to return home on a high. There would be no need to treat any belief as either true or false again. And even though I didn't need to believe that thought, it was certainly liberating.

The Direct Path and Emptiness
by Sandra Pippa

❝ The case of the direct path and emptiness teachings is an interesting example of two views that overlap to some extent. They appear to have different goals, one awareness, the other Emptiness, and it's possible to conflate the two goals, which would be a mistake. But both paths lead to liberation from the belief of a separate personal existence, and both use techniques of self-inquiry to get there. ❞

From advaita to emptiness teachings

I've known about the direct path for a long time, but I chose not to be a follower when I put my Advaita books on the shelf more than a decade ago. I'd been a devoted student of Vedanta[38] for many years but switched to Buddhism and the emptiness teachings,[39] a study that changed my life and is still going strong.

I would eventually get a feel for the direct path, and sort out what it was that made me question absolute values like *Sat, Chit, Ananda.*[40] But I'd need to struggle and I'd need to learn a lot more about what it means to inquire into the nature of things, myself included.

Why did I turn away from a teaching I dearly loved to

---

38. Vedanta: one of the six schools of Indian philosophy, based on ancient texts including the Upanishads, Vedanta includes living traditions such as Advaita Vedanta (nondualism), qualified nondualism and dualism.
39. Emptiness: "On the one hand, Sunyata [emptiness] is a very profound dimension of reality—the key to the supremely joyful state of complete freedom. Yet on the other, it is simply the uncontrived way things are, free from labels and reification. It is part of the natural state of everything". Goode, G. and Sander, T. (2016) *Emptiness and Joyful Freedom*, Non-Duality Press
40. *Sat Chit Ananda*: literally truth, consciousness, bliss

embrace a philosophy that doesn't even recognize the one true Self? Was this a conscious move or an intuitive decision?

By intuition people usually mean a sense of knowing something whose source is mysterious. My own take on intuition includes a *déjà-vu* sense that what's being experienced is related to something I'd learned long ago but had forgotten. I don't usually think of a decision as intuitive at the time I make it. Often enough, I only realize that after the fact, sometimes years later.

Intuition can be alluring and it got hold of me one night back in the 1980s. I went to attend a lecture on philosophy that was being held in a mansion on the Upper East Side of Manhattan. I followed the receptionist to a majestic room with a person up front who was speaking about unusual things. The message was that we are all more than just connected: we are the same being. The speaker was talking about the Atman,[41] and I was smitten. I left the building starry-eyed that night. Walking on Lexington Avenue to the subway back to Brooklyn was like walking on air.

I returned again and again to that place and became one among many dedicated students at The School of Practical Philosophy. I loved the teaching. The people there became family and we studied and practiced together for years. We read the Gita,[42] studied the Upanishads,[43] practiced calligraphy, and worked with attention exercises. We came to weekly classes and participated in "service," attended retreats, and meditated twice daily. All was done with the goal of reconnecting to the source of our true nature: knowledge, truth, and bliss. I'm

---

41. Atman: the individual "soul", self or essence which is at one with the universal principle or Brahman.
42. The Bhagavad Gita, known as "The Gita", is a Hindu text over 2,000 years old. As part of the epic Mahabharata it sets out a synthesis of approaches to the conduct of life, spirituality and liberation.
43. The Upanishads are influential Indian spiritual/philosophical texts, some dating back 2,500 years.

happy I followed my gut feeling, as what I learned there about nonduality set me on a course I don't regret.

Bumps in the road

That's not to say that all was well at The School in those days. I found out there were prices to pay for this teaching of liberation. I remember the day the women were each called in for an interview with the head of our New York School. I sat stiff in my small chair, apprehensive before this tall man at his big desk while he asked me personal questions like whether I'd ever had an abortion. He admonished me to always surrender to my husband and "through The School to the Absolute." The women were taught in classes separate from the men, who were given secret, "higher" teachings that the women weren't privy to. Women were encouraged to leave careers and stay home with children. One of my best friends, a high-spirited and gifted woman, was getting up daily at 4:00 a.m. to iron her husband's underwear!

Why did we put up with that? I admit that back then I wasn't equipped to challenge the blatant sexist attitudes and behaviors rampant there. I was uncomfortable at times, but mostly I was clueless and content to be reading and studying the ancient scriptures. I trusted those higher up in The School who said that the only way to make progress was to practice more, to work harder, and to keep doing what I was told. I didn't see that some of the bad feelings and thoughts I had about myself were not just engendered by the patriarchal system, the hierarchy in place in that institution, but were also reinforced by it. Lucky for me a rebel would take up residence next to the softy in my naive heart.

After I'd been at Philosophy School for several years, a day school was created as instructed by the higher-ups in London so the dream of providing a place where youngsters could grow up with this philosophy could finally come true. We were persuaded to take our children out of the schools they were in and bring them over to the new day school, and that's what many of us did.

It seemed like a wonderful opportunity, but there were bumps in the road. One day our drive into Manhattan was slow due to an accident on the highway, and I was nervous that our six-year-old would be late for school. When I walked him into his class, his teacher glared at us and sternly instructed our son to go to the side of the room and wait. I realized my boy was being singled out,and would be punished for being late. Why? Why not welcome an innocent one with a smile? A lot of feelings and ideas came to the surface. I thought about all the times I'd been made to feel miserable there because of a misguided sense of privilege. Hurting my child was the last straw.

We made our exit shortly after that. I found out later our son was shamed and made to stand alone before the rest of his classmates and explain to them why he was leaving. He cried himself to sleep for weeks. I never quite forgave myself for putting him through that, and I'll never know if he ever really got over it. It's been hard to forgive the self-righteous man who took it upon himself to inflict pain on so many, especially little ones, in the name of the glorified Self.

Searching for the self

Leaving The School of Practical Philosophy was like moving to a foreign country. There was a rule in place that members weren't to associate with people who dropped out. We were shunned, we were traitors! Or worse, lost souls. It was a struggle, but there was solace in finding nondual teachings alive and well on the outside. I found the world of satsangs in New York City. It was an exciting time.

As much as I liked meeting teachers like Francis Lucille and Wayne Liquorman, the frustration I found at Philosophy School accompanied me when I left. I may have had dazzling insights at times, but I could not connect all the way with the teaching, could not access my Self. *Neti neti* [44] was becoming, "not this, not this, thou art that something over there, stretch, reach for it, you can do it!...No wait, it's right here, so twist around back..."

Not only that, I kept running into the problem of teachers getting in the way of teaching.

I encountered a "my way or the highway" mentality more than once or twice at satsangs where the guy at the front of the room clearly enjoyed being revered in the eyes of some at the expense of others.

But I kept reading. I read books on Zen, books on awareness, book after book. I learned about Sri Atmananda from a friend, and I read through the two soft blue booklets *Atma Darshan* and *Atma Nivriti*.[45] Here was a different take on a teaching I'd been following and practicing for many years. Maybe I'd finally found the right approach, a systematic way that would straighten things out for me.

The Middle Way

Right about the same time I discovered the texts of the great Tibetan interpreters of Buddha and began to have discussions with friends about The Middle Way. One day while reading a book on the emptiness teachings I could practically hear the concept of dependent origination, the understanding that nothing exists independently of other things, sink down and click into place. I felt a chill ripple across my skin. Something powerful and heavenly was at work. It felt like I was engaged to a person I'd known all my life, but on the eve of my wedding I

---

44. *Neti neti* is a Sanskrit expression which means "not this, not this." In Hinduism, particularly Advaita Vedanta, it is used as a meditation that aims to distinguish between the impermanent, relative world of *Maya* and the eternal Absolute *Brahman*.
45. See Reading List p.160

had met someone else, my soulmate.

The emptiness teachings had a profound effect on my life. The draining effort to understand was replaced with a surprising new way of seeing. It meant that things I take as substantial like my family, my life, even the present moment, are actually wrongly perceived. My tendency to believe in some deep way that all things exist in and of themselves was being replaced by seeing no unique self in any object, idea, or feeling. That understanding applied to my seeking, to my self, and to awareness, too. And it came with a relaxing of the expectation for things to be a certain way. Not only was this a fascinating ancient teaching that made perfect sense, I'd found a springboard into a new world that included experiencing not just philosophy, art, and literature, but also my everyday life in ways that were creative and endless.

The struggle to understand a way to be at one with myself loosened its grip once the concept of dependent arising settled in. No ultimate essence to be, to see, or to understand. We go looking for an object, or a self, and we find its absence—an absence that still allows a thing to exist, but in what emptiness teachings call a "conventional" way. I came to see conventional existence as incredibly meaningful and precious because that's all there is. All things depend on other things in order just to be. This connection is crucial but fragile and fleeting. If a rose, a person, or a mountain had ultimate existence in the way we usually think they do, everything would be static. Nothing could unfold, grow, or change.

You could say that how it came about that I turned away from the awareness teachings and the direct path is all wrapped up in circumstances and timing. There was no conscious decision on my part to leave one teaching and take up another. But looking back, I can see that something about Atmananda and his teachings reminded me of the downside of my days at The School of Practical Philosophy. There was that striking photo of Atmananda Krishna Menon in *Atma Darshan*, sitting cross-legged, so still, so stern. A beautiful patriarch. One more man looking straight at me telling me what's what.

Patriarchal sexism

My views continue to clarify as to how the past seems to affect the way things unfold. I look at how people treat each other, the privileges they assume. A friend recently sent me a book about two people I'd become acquainted with back in my Philosophy School days. The book is titled *The Power Within*,[46] by Dorine Tolley. It tells the story of Leon MacLaren, a British gentleman who founded our Philosophy School headquartered in England. His teaching derived from Gurdjieff and Ouspensky, then ultimately HH Santananda Saraswati, Shankaracharya of the Northern Seat of the four centers for Vedic teaching in India, established by Adi Shankara around 800 A.D.

Dorine Tolley was years younger than Mr. MacLaren and was his constant companion from the time she was barely 20 years old in 1973 until his death in 1994. Her book is about their lives, their round-the-world trips visiting and managing the various schools opened under Mr. MacLaren's guidance. His ability to disseminate the perennial teaching to thousands of others is legendary. Dorine saw greatness in Mr. MacLaren, felt it her duty to serve him, and did not want to let him down when he clearly valued her highly and needed her badly. They were not a married couple. Dorine was Mr. MacLaren's aide, and in the book she portrays herself as someone who cherished and honored the 20 years she spent at the side of this remarkable man.

But there is an undercurrent of sadness in the tale. The difficulty leaving family and friends in Holland to travel and care for this person was profound for Dorine, but she was compelled by the pressure and the desire to be of service. Even though Mr.

---

46. Tolley, D. (2009) *The Power Within*, BookSurge

MacLaren immensely appreciated her company and her talents, it was hard to let go of the desire to attend university, to forgo a family of her own, to give up choosing her own life.

She writes about visiting the many Philosophy Schools in far-away countries and how the women would gather around her to ask questions when she arrived. They told her about feeling cast aside, ignored because they were female. Living conditions that were at times dismal and years of sleepless nights on call 24/7 to this man took a toll on her health. And then there's the time Mr. MacLaren slapped her across the face after she expressed homesickness at Christmas time.

I recently watched a little film online, *All About Nothing*,[47] by a Dutchman named Paul Smit. It's a well intentioned mishmash of vignettes meant to edify us on the virtues of nondual teachings. While the male characters in the piece are mostly brilliant and thoughtful, the females, save for one older woman, are portrayed as shallow dimwits.

I was appalled watching that movie, as were the savvy friends who told me about it. What's shocking is how many people commented in glowing terms about the film. They were oblivious to the sexist attitude that's so clear to me and my friends. And then there are the posts, videos, jokes, and photos that demean women that come up in Facebook groups often, even where the focus is on nondual teachings.

Liberation from the one thing that everything points to

By now it might seem that I was put off the direct path and Advaita teachings because of the patriarchal and sexist views I encountered while following them. I could make a case for those views being embedded in the teaching itself. I think there are dangers in paths that posit one thing that everything points to,

---

47. https://tinyurl.com/y9ea2wf5 [accessed 28 Nov 2018]

whether it's an Atman, the Absolute, or awareness. Direct-path teachings state that consciousness alone is immune to change. All else is referred to as objects.

The passages in Atmananda's books and notes that clarify the difference between consciousness and the things that appear to it are beautiful, but a superficial reading that privileges consciousness on high, and considers bodies, feelings and so forth, as mere categories of delusion, can be tricky. Can I stand as awareness when my child is missing for 24 hours? When I learn my precious new friend was sexually assaulted?

Nondual teachings can be seen to discount minds, bodies, thoughts, and feelings in favor of an overarching something else. Essentialist teachings mirror the age-old concept of a supreme authority that's been in place in every aspect of society and culture we know: family, religion, government, and everything in between.

I think the fact that the emptiness teachings offer no reference to a thing, either man or god, concept or substance, that all things lead back to was liberating for me, even if the process was instinctive when I first encountered the teaching. Objects, people, and things are all seen as the same in emptiness teachings, meaning they lack inherent existence. That levels the playing field from the get-go: no ultimate consciousness to look back to—no father image, either. No one to answer to or to worry about pleasing.

I first learned about emptiness teachings by way of the Madhyamaka School but went on to study other Buddhist teachings, including Vipassana, Theravada, and Zen. I didn't find sexist and patriarchal elements in the sanghas and temples during my visits or in conversations with friends I made there. I did encounter a more diverse population of people of color and gender than I did in the Advaita groups I attended. I learned practices like *metta*, the loving-kindness meditation, and found a sense of inclusiveness, ease, and comfort.

Emptiness and compassion

All of this points to one of the basic tenets of Buddhism, the concept of compassion. It's built into the teaching and is a major focus of most schools of Buddhist thought. All beings are suffering and looking for a way out. Not one of us is free from the pain of suffering. Therefore, compassion for others is taught. If I consider the suffering of countless others compared to the suffering of this one single person, me, maybe I can get to an understanding of having compassion for others, to consider them even before myself.

I learned that the concept of compassion works in tandem with the concept of the two truths. The ultimate truth of our nature is emptiness. But as conventional beings we do exist, dependent on conditions. In fact, since conventional beings are the only ones that do exist, we're all deserving of love, compassion, and understanding.

There's a wonderful irony in the way emptiness, a teaching that posits a lack of ultimate existence, can seem so inclusive, welcoming, and free. What I absorbed from my experience and study of Buddhism and emptiness teachings created an impression of kindness and equanimity and a distinct lack of authoritarian views.

So when I look at these two paths and my own experiences, I have to ask: are nondual teachings sexist and patriarchal while Buddhist teachings aren't? It can seem that way, and my experiences point to that. But others have different experiences that create impressions that influence their actions and propel their lives. And I have to consider the strong feminists, men and women both, who love and practice nondual teachings with integrity and self-awareness. Some are among the most brilliant and admirable people I know. And there are many stories of Buddhist teachers who've taken advantage of women in their sanghas in ways that are reprehensible.

Liberation from struggling to find the "right path"

Unfortunately, sexist and patriarchal ways are alive and well just about everywhere. My heart aches for the women and girls who are abused because of these attitudes and beliefs. Still, I have to remember that these ways and behaviors are dependent arisings; they occur because of causes and conditions. And that means they can change.

They can change from a painful past and present to a future that's safer, kinder, and better—not just for women, but for society in general. Sexism doesn't exist anywhere, including in nondual teachings, in an intrinsic way. But that doesn't mean that it doesn't cause harm. One of the most valuable insights the concept of emptiness provided for me is that knowing there isn't anything final to attain or to land on applies to emptiness itself—meaning that nothing can be seen as uniquely right or wrong, good or bad, including paths and teachings. Ironically, I harbored a vague hypocrisy for longer than I realized, a thought that I'd found the "right" path and that teachings espousing an ultimate, like Brahman[48] or awareness, didn't point to the way we really are. The bias was subtle and it took a while for it to fade. When the implications of that understanding finally dawned, it was like a rising sun that never sets.

And it opened the door wider to an interest in other teachings. I like to bow to a lovely Buddha that sits on a shelf next to a sculpture of Ganesha, which is near a statue of the Ksitigarbha Bodhisattva in my living room. I recently acquired a connection to the Holy Mother, and I like to hold a rosary when I meditate. It might seem confusing, even silly, but it isn't to me. I love these icons and rituals, and each one of them has a particular usefulness and meaning for me. Rather than causing any break

---

48. *Brahman*: in Hinduism, the unchanging eternal reality that includes and subsumes all appearances. The Absolute.

in devotion or scattering of sensibility, this practice makes me feel safe, comfortable, focused, and open.

Rediscovering the direct path in light of emptiness teachings

When the opportunity came up not long ago to take another look at the direct path, I figured, why not get reacquainted, like old friends who'd had a falling out. My books on the direct path came down from the shelf and new ones were added. As I read and re-read these books I had a desire to explore a direct version of a teaching I'd set aside long ago.

I decided to follow some of the practices and found I can still connect with the beauty of Advaitic teachings and what I learned from them all those years ago. But this inquiry is direct and precise, not incomplete and vague as it often seemed when I practiced back then. I can stand as awareness and see how sensations like piercing grief and deep joy rise up and disappear in consciousness in the same way as the body and mind that seem so connected to them.

I have an affinity for the Heart Opener,[49] and I see the value of challenging the separate existence of the apparent objects of my senses. As I work my way through these exercises, from the world to body and mind, I notice there's been a tendency to see some of those arisings as things to set aside or as objects that are not quite good enough to be "awareness." Now I begin to see that of course they are a part of awareness. Everything is included. Nothing gets left out. There's wholeness then, and peace.

Direct path and emptiness together

Having an interest in these two paths brings up a few other questions, such as whether a person can be devoted to more than one teaching. Are paths like emptiness teachings and the

49. See Appendix p.163

direct path mutually exclusive? Do these paths lead to the same end?

There's an interesting debate as to the importance and relevance of ultimate goals in various religions and philosophical paths. I like the radical approach of S. Mark Heim in his book *Salvations*[50], where he proposes a pluralistic perspective that embraces the value of another teaching while maintaining a preference for one's own tradition and ultimate goal. Paths don't need to be differing ways of relating to the same reality. Some paths may lead to the same ultimate end, and some may not. Religions and philosophic paths can have their own truths and their own ways of fulfilling them, and can even be open to their adherents participating in another spiritual view.

The case of the direct path and emptiness teachings is an interesting example of two views that overlap to some extent. They appear to have different goals, one awareness, the other Emptiness, and it's possible to conflate the two goals, which would be a mistake. But both paths lead to liberation from the belief in a separate personal existence, and both use techniques of self-inquiry to get there.

I like looking into the direct path a little deeper than I'd considered up until now because having experiences of other possible ways I exist confirms firsthand that there isn't just one way. I think a person can follow more than one teaching if there is respect for practices, history, and beliefs, in order to understand a path's character. I have a new interest in direct-path teachings, but I would never turn away from emptiness teachings, because for me, that would be like trying to unlearn how to speak or deciding I don't need food or water anymore.

I don't think awareness teachings are for everyone. In my opinion there are aspects of nondual paths that make them susceptible to dogmatic tendencies, but they obviously can be

50. Heim, S.M. (1995) *Salvations: Truth and Difference in Religion*, Orbis Books

taught and experienced in a way that steers clear of those pitfalls. In my case, I was drawn to both awareness teachings and emptiness teachings in ways that seemed natural at the time, and I'm convinced that either path can serve as a source of deep knowledge and joy for those who follow them.

And intuition? Is that what steered me away from one teaching and toward another when the timing was right? Intuition could be about connecting to something known before and forgotten, or maybe to what will be known in the future. I just read that Kierkegaard suggested that life must be understood backwards, but lived forwards. When I look back I have regrets. I wish I'd made better decisions and studied harder. I wish I'd been a more compassionate person and contributed more. There's been sorrow, but there's been so much love, and there's been understanding, too.

So whatever intuition is—a word, a cliché, an arising to witnessing awareness—I like it when it shows up. I like the jolt of recognition, the magnetic pull that tells me to pay attention even when I don't know why I should right then. I will likely keep trusting those sensations, deconstruct them when I can, and keep living forward, like Kierkegaard said. And I'll remind myself that understanding has many different ways of unfolding, and fortunately I don't have to unravel every single mystery that comes along.

Berkeley and Blake: An Extended Look at Objectivity
by John Lamont-Black

"Whether understood as the products of perceptual triangulation or whatever, objects can still have meaning as things of beauty and utility and lots more besides, but we don't have to believe that they are fundamentally existent as separate entities. And if they aren't fundamentally separate or even extant...then are we?"

The cliffs of objectivity

Many years ago, around the time I was deciding whether to study science or engineering, I set out for a long walk in the direction of the coast to mull over this impending decision. Somewhere beneath the towering cliffs came an idea: "I want to know the true nature and structure of reality." Even then I smiled at the pomposity of the suggestion, but I had to admit that it was the kind of thing a scientist might say.

The Seven Sisters cliffs are one of Britain's most iconic landscapes. Stretching over 10 miles and rising to a height of over 160 metres above sea level, the swathe of bright white vertical chalk forms a stark visual and topographical disconnect between the gently textured surfaces of green fields and the blue-gray sea. This part of the coast is a beautiful and potentially dangerous place.

To some, these cliffs represent the quintessential border of England, and they have inspired film directors and painters towards high art, and some politicians towards base nationalism. To thousands of birds and millions of invertebrates, the nooks and crannies provide homes. To mercifully few, such as shipwrecked sailors, reckless climbers, and even despairing souls, these cliffs are places of death.

The cliffs have been featured in poems, paintings, and

films over the centuries, but what they signify depends on who is doing the looking. On this theme of perspective, the eighteenth-century English poet, artist, and mystic William Blake observed:

> I see Every thing I paint In This World, but Every body does not see alike... The tree which moves some to tears of joy is in the Eyes of others only a Green thing that stands in the way... As a man is, So he Sees.[51]

"As a man is, So he Sees." So indeed! To me on that afternoon, these cliffs were something complete, absorbing, joyful. Scientifically (geologically) understood, from the smallest nanoscopic coccolith to piles of carbonate mud hundreds of metres thick filling continental-scale tectonic sedimentary basins, they represented a local chapter in the origin and history of our planet and of all life upon it. Engineering, I thought, might be fine, but seriously, why would I want to study anything besides geology?

As it turned out, I have spent much of my working life as a scientist working closely with engineers; observing phenomena and seeking to explain their causal origins and predict their effects. Below I look at what happens when this habit of seeking explanations for things bumps up against objectivity itself.

The direct path

The basic model of dualism is that of a subject relating to an object. In the model of common-sense reality, this means a subject (me) knowing or experiencing by some means (thinking, sensing, perceiving) an object of some sort (mental, physical, emotional). Most of the time such a way of knowing is fine, but short moments or extended periods of sadness, suffering,

---

51. Letter from William Blake to Reverend John Trusler, 23 August 1799

or unhappiness seem to be linked by an amplified awareness of myself as separate or even isolated. The direct path has helped me to see in detail how I experience objectivity, to question the fundamental assumptions of separation, and therefore to gain insight into unhappiness.

I approached the direct path a bit like a scientist might; that is, by experiment and observation to test hypotheses, of which there seemed to be two. The first is that all we know of objects is our perceptions of them. The second is that there is no real separation between what we call perceptions and awareness, or that with which perceptions (and all things) are known.

For most of us when we investigate our perceptions of touch, taste and smell, we find them to be intimate experiences, right here and now. However, perceptions with a spatial component such as hearing and especially vision (the main theme discussed herein) seem to include real and direct evidence of separation between me and the object being perceived. Despite much enquiry for the purpose of deconstructing visual objects, I'd find that when I opened my eyes, the world would jump "out there" distinctly and repetitiously. This seemed to me to be self-evident and incontrovertible: physical objects are real, and part of their reality is their separation-defining distance from me.

The direct-path teaching, like other nondual investigations, insisted on the primacy of direct experience: raw perceptions and the resultant percepts, rather than concepts. I was sure that I was being true to this, but there seemed no getting around it: when I opened my eyes the world really jumped out there!

Like an irate fly newly arrived at a window, I buzzed against the idea that if vision is just a perception like the others, then it should permit direct understanding of the lack of separation between me and these sensations: vision and the objects seen should be intimate like taste and touch. But this was not the case: when the world jumped out there, the distinct feeling of distance seemed to confirm the independence of objects at a distance as the causes of my perceptions. I felt centred and fixed like the hub of a bicycle wheel with spokes of vision radiating out to distant objects.

I read widely around the issue, inquiring into ideas such as the container metaphor of objects *in* awareness and awareness *in* the body. Investigation of the objectivity/distance issue through other approaches such as direct pointing seemed flawed because their questions seemed to lack coherence, for instance asking, "What distance is that object from you, who are awareness?" or "Where is the boundary between you, awareness, and that object?" Such queries introduced the very thing they were seeking to show as illusory, and to me, such questions were about as helpful as suggesting, "Don't think of a pink elephant!"

I was aware from the start that the questions assumed the existence of the very thing they were questioning and were thus to a degree rhetorical. However, I was totally unaware of the strength and over-confidence of the realist-materialist-literalist mind-set of my upbringing and schooling, which asserted and took for granted that things can always be worked out.

At the end of several frustrating months, I took some time out from investigations, to just forget about enquiry for a while.

Berkeley

I returned refreshed and less hurried to inquire once again into physical objectivity and distance and was directed to the writings of the eighteenth-century priest and philosopher George Berkeley. He proved to be a great help, not because of any worldview or metaphysics he propounded, but rather because of the elegance of his method, which to the empirical scientist in me appeared like a welcoming face at the door of enquiry.

Berkeley stressed the importance of what he called "immediate" experience, by which he meant unmediated by thought, which is synonymous with the direct path's direct experience. In practice, it means attending only to the actual information of the senses without the overlay of thinking. In the introduction to his *Principles of Human Knowledge*[52] he wrote:

> ...I earnestly desire that every one would use his utmost endeavours to attain to a clear and naked view of the ideas he would consider, by separating them from all that varnish and mist of words, which so fatally blinds the judgement...Unless we take care to clear the first principles of knowledge from the incumbrances and delusions of words, we may make infinite reasonings upon them to no purpose. We may deduce consequences, and never be the wiser.

In attending to experience with the above in mind, he distinguished perceptual objects, or percepts of the senses, from the common-sense physical objects that are perceived. Berkeley challenged the common-sense view of objectivity, which, under the leadership of scientific materialism, asserted that physical objects are made of matter, which is what we actually perceive.

Berkeley and objects

Berkeley's way of looking had two key insights:

1) Direct or immediate experience is not about anything—it's just raw experience. And if we look into that raw experience, the best we can say about it is that it appears as ideas in the mind.
2) All we know of the world are those ideas, and we never come into direct contact with an object in itself.

52. Berkeley, T (1734) *A Treatise on the Principles of Human Knowledge*, Hackett Publishing (Winkler, K. ed, 1982)

These insights were not dismissing common-sense experience as illusory, but rather re-contextualizing it as mind, or arising in awareness, rather than matter. Further, they highlighted in a startlingly clear manner that experience "about" physical objects only makes sense in the context or framework of physical objectivity; the corollary being that physical objectivity requires the existence of physical objects to establish or set the context.

The circularity was stunning! I immediately recognized the revolving thought patterns of an addict. Many years ago when trying to quit smoking I wondered, "Why do I want a cigarette?" The comically obvious answer was "Because it relieves the craving for a cigarette." That was all! Relief of craving was the only benefit, and it made sense only within the context of addictive smoking, that is to say... craving.

It was dawning on me that such is the case with physical objectivity. Why do I believe in discrete physical objects? Because discrete objects make sense of this belief. And Berkeley revealed it to be a belief. I have never actually come into contact with an object in itself.

Berkeley and distance

Berkeley's treatment of perception helped me to better understand the perceptual intimacy that I had discovered experientially with tasting, touching, and smelling. Regarding vision, I had made some small progress, and could accept intellectually or in principle that all I might know of a visual object was an idea in the mind (or arising in awareness). But the convincing character of distance seemed to undermine these insights. There was just something about distance that felt so real. It was clearly a sticking point: I needed to have a long hard look at what I understood by "distance."

In the *Three Dialogues*[53] Berkeley introduces three ways to consider objects at a distance:

1) First, he observes that distance is common to both the waking and dreaming states, concluding that we cannot be sure that the experience of distance in the waking state really relates to what we think of as spatial separation of objects.

2) Next, he reminds us of the common-sense view that an object appears to get bigger as we approach it. But he asks, if the object could really get bigger, what would that even mean? He points out that by attending to vision, we realize that we do not see an enlarging physical object, or a similarly changing visual percept; rather, our experiences are perhaps better described as multiple visual percepts. He posits that we learn to associate the experience of a succession of visual percepts with the experience of a succession of bodily feelings and sensations in the context of physical movement, such as walking towards an object. The regular association of these and similar object pairs gives rise to what we have learned to call extension and distance.

3) Finally, he asks, "But to make it more plain: isn't distance a line running out from the eye?" It can be conceived this way, but such a line cannot be seen; therefore distance is not an object of direct experience. In conclusion he concedes with respect to distance, "Even if it were truly perceived by the mind [which it is not] it still wouldn't follow that it existed outside the mind."

Berkeley is pointing out that distance is not directly experienced,

53. Berkeley, G. (1713) *Three Dialogues between Hylas and Philonous.*

but rather involves vision and kinaesthetic experiences - seeing and "feeling" in association with each other.

A penny dropped... distance *feels* so real because it's not just vision: *feelings* are involved too.[54] If you stand beneath a towering cliff, or especially at the top, it becomes clear that the role of feeling in the body is no longer a matter of debate!

These conclusions had derived from work begun as part of Berkeley's doctoral thesis and published as his *New Theory of Vision* (1709). Here he conducts a thought experiment to explore the interdependence of sight, touch, and objectivity. He considers a disembodied intelligence that only possesses, and has only ever possessed, vision:

> "153.....consider the case of an intelligence, or unbodied spirit, which is supposed to see perfectly well, to have a clear perception of the proper and immediate objects of sight, but to have no sense of touch...

> 154. First, then, it is certain the aforesaid intelligence could have no idea of a solid, or quantity of three dimensions, which followeth from its not having any idea of distance. We indeed are prone to think that we have by sight the ideas of space and solids, which ariseth from our imagining that we do, strictly speaking, see distance and some parts of an object at a greater distance than others; which hath been demonstrated to be the effect of the experience we have had, what ideas of touch are connected with such and such ideas attending vision: but the intelligence here spoken of is supposed to have no experience of touch. He would not, therefore, judge as

---

54. For the avoidance of doubt herein I am using the definition that sensations = sense perceptions of the objects of the world; feelings = sense perceptions in the body, e.g. kinaesthetic, sensorimotors proprioceptive, pain, pressure and so forth; emotions = combination of feelings + thoughts.

we do, nor have any idea of distance, outness, or profundity [depth], nor consequently of space or body, either immediately or by suggestion."

Berkeley concludes that, without the tactile sense (upon which extension and therefore distance rely), the disembodied intelligence would have no means of defining objects in its (uniquely visual) experience. This conclusion made perfect sense to me, and I wondered if I could verify it for myself.

Colour and form

When we speak of visual objects, we often refer to colour and shape (form). It seemed obvious to me that I can see an object that has colour, has shape, and is over there. Now, colour may be characterized by descriptors such as hue, saturation, and brightness, but what about shape? Following Berkeley, and his suggestion that a single unaccompanied perceptual modality would be insufficient to define an object, I wondered if there might not be a distinction to be drawn between these two facets of visual experience. And furthermore if there really are, or even can be, *two* facets of this thing I call vision. And if so, what would that even mean?

As is the direct-path way, I asked simple questions and looked for experiential answers.

With respect to vision, can there be colour without shape? The answer appeared to be yes. Can there be shape without colour? Visual evidence would indicate no. By this reckoning colour is fundamental to vision but shape is not, i.e. shape isn't entirely visual in the same way that colour seems to be. But is that true?

I found that I do not see any physical objects that are purely colourful, i.e. a visual experience of an "object" that comprises colour but has no shape. Investigating form, such as the shape of a white cloud in the blue sky, I explore both the outline against the background blue and the billowing internal lobes. Following the hint in Berkeley and paying close attention to bodily sensations, I noticed faint and subtle kinaesthetic movements and feelings, little more than ghostly gestures associated with tracing the outline and sculpting the form.

In a manner similar to Berkeley's observation on the experience of distance and extension in dreaming, I explored the experience of simple imagination. For example, I visualized a simple shape, in this case a yellow square against a black background. Exploring this I noticed that it was accompanied by subtle tactile stroking of the imaginary sides and cresting of the corners. Similarly, I tried to consider with purely kinaesthetic imagination, or "kinaesation," a purely tactile square, but it proved almost impossible to exclude associated subtle visualizations. These two senses appear repeatedly and faithfully associated with each other and combine in the context of an object.

These were new experiences, or at least it seemed that way. Charmed and enticed by the discovery, I went on the hunt for more.

Sitting one day at my desk watching a delivery at a neighbour's house, I saw the driver walk up the path, deliver the package, return to his vehicle, and depart. I noticed that these visually emphasized interpretations were accompanied by what I'd call subtle kinaesthetic gestures of reaching and extension— quite literally a faint bodily sense of movement associated with watching the postman advance up the path. Here was the silent partner of visual distance. It was real, I felt it, and I was excited by the discovery!

Multiple small insights followed. I expanded this to looking at edges, surfaces, and volumes—cables, mantelpieces, brickwork, sculptures, and landscapes. Each and every time, the main visual feast was enlivened by subtle, invisible kinaesthetic condiments.

At the time I thought that this was some kind of major breakthrough! Gone was the frustration of the idea of no distance. Distance was and remained real, but it was not what I'd always thought it to be. I realized that distance was not out there in 3-D space, but in experience it arose as a seeing with feeling. The kinaesthetic feeling that arises with, or is cued by, vision organizes colours as shapes and is congruent with the idea of objectivity.

Very quickly I realized that it was no longer a problem that when I opened my eyes the world jumped out there. Yes, it did. Of course it did! But it didn't jump *into pre-existing space*; distance itself is the combination of seeing and the feeling of reaching or extension. The nature of what I knew as distance was visual-kinaesthetic, not dimensional. I had found Berkeley's "line running out from the eye," which was unseen and felt rather than inferred and geometrical.

Distance, proximity, closeness, and separation were no longer making the same sense that they once had. "Here" and "there" graduated from referring strictly to a location in space to taking on more evocative meanings, as combinations of intimate experiences of vision and feeling.

Through Berkeley I had confirmed that, to define an object, at least two lines of evidence are required—for example, visual and kinaesthetic. I tagged this as "triangulation." Furthermore, when two or more senses seem to agree about the existence of an object, the reality effect is increased. The reality effect is a kind of conviction about the existence of a real object. It is increased because we think that our experiences can't be just the artifacts of one sense. And we're right, sort of...

We see something at a distance. Firstly, just to delineate its outline and shape, subtle kinaesthetic senses are at work. Then even without actually reaching out and touching the object, the subtle kinaesthetic (extension) sense cued from vision serves as a proxy for independent evidence, and together they combine as distance. Such cues emerge from over a lifetime of learning associations. It is as if perception is cheating: introducing its own supporting evidence and claiming an independent origin for it!

At first blush, then, it seems that I can see an object, which has shape and has colour and is over there. But: I know nothing of the object apart from the ideas of shape and colour; colour and shape are inseparable in the context of an object; and I know nothing of distance without the idea of objectivity and kinaesthetic extension. Everything depends on everything else.

A note on time

Part of my direct-path enquiry included an exploration of language and the ways in which we express ourselves. This illustrated the central role of metaphor. It is much more important than merely a creative mode of expression: we also describe, investigate and compare with metaphor. Many of the metaphors we think with are based on the ideas of distance and space, which I'd come to understand as combinations of vision and kinaesthetic feeling. And just as for distance, we have no way of directly sensing time, but we make it real by association.

In thinking about time we invariably use some form of non-temporal metaphor. The majority of time metaphors are spatial and examples of the relative movement of an observer and an object known as an event—for example, "The summer seems to be zooming by," or "There's going to be trouble down the road."

Even saying "I'll see you *in* five minutes" or "I'll meet you *at* two" defines a location, in or at. There is nothing inherently temporal about these. Even when the hour hand passes over the 2, it's a spatial correlation.

Following a line of enquiry similar to that followed for physical objects into how I think about time revealed that spatial representation (and for me that means visualization-kinaesation) is central to my experience. I wondered if space and time might be similarly visio-kinaesthetically triangulated. Perhaps I triangulate motion (kinaesthetic) and events (concepts) and appear to come up with time in a similar way that I seem to do so for motion (kinaesthetic) and objects (percepts) for space, such that:

- ❖ Distance (space) is the combination of visual objects and kinaesthetic cues in the context of physical objects (one of which might be me, here).

- ❖ Duration (time) is the combination of visual and kinaesthetic cues in the context of conceptual events (one of which might be me, now).

It matters not whether an object is considered primary or cued; all arise in direct experience as awareness and are thus known without, and prior to, any sense of location. The ideas of here (in space) and now (in time) might just be constructed points of view that provide one-half of the contexts within which space and time make sense, but are not given in either direct or cued experience.

The myth of triangulation

When I understood that kinaesthetic experience cues the idea of seen distance and perhaps also time, it started to become clear that visual-tactile/extension elements seem to be built into the way I think via innumerable spatially referenced metaphors—for example, "directing attention," a sensation "arising," or even "in" thinking "about" a problem, and "arriving at" a solution. The examples are legion. And these metaphors are not simply rhetorical devices but rather in my own investigated experience have subtle physical-perceptual embodiments. Fleeting and subtle visual and associated kinaesthetic sensations are seen to accompany even abstract concepts such as mental arithmetic, planning a diary, considering deep geological time, or notions of relationship and history, or in the appreciation of music.

Triangulations seemed to be everywhere. I imagined complex networks of triangulated ideas and triangles within triangles. It was tantalizing, and it felt like I was making, or was on the edge of making, major progress in explaining objectivity. I thought I might be on the way to explaining the origins of space and time in my experience. This, unsurprisingly, had the whiff of pomposity once again. So I inspected triangulation itself.

As a model for explaining the origin of objects, triangulation doesn't stand. And it falls for two main reasons:

1) All the objects or arisings, whatever their nature, can be seen as awareness through the investigations organized within the direct path. For example, remove awareness from one's knowing an object: what remains? Add something that is not awareness to one's knowing of an object: what changes? Nothing on both counts.

2) The idea of triangulation can be shown to lack coherency in principle because:

   a) We cannot in our immediate direct experience know more than one thing at a time. Any declaration that asserts that we can do so, becomes itself what is known. Thus we can never actually see the "triangle" so conceived (we cannot see all three points) as a whole in itself. Such would surely be the most basic and minimum requirement of the triangulation model. For example, when I listen to music or gaze over a landscape, experience is whole. It is only a thought that purports to carve up experience into pieces and then another thought that tries to relate the pieces to each other.

b) In the triangulation model or context, each corner represents an object and each side represents a relationship. All sides are dependent on corners and all corners are dependent on sides: no single object can ever be confirmed independently.

c) The very idea that we can even make connections between vertices implies the context of planar geometry such that triangulation is a context within a context, thus its ability to explain objectivity as fundamental is questionable.

For me this incoherency is illustrated beautifully in many of the works of M. C. Escher and, in its simplest form, the Penrose Triangle. Originally created by Oscar Reutersvärd in 1934, it was popularized in the 1950s by father and son Lionel and Roger Penrose, who described it as "impossibility in its purest form."

The Penrose Triangle

As a whole the lines themselves create an interesting and pleasing view. But when we try to interpret them in terms of a coherent structure—that is to say, to put them in a 3-D context rather than just a pleasing view—something interesting happens. Individually each corner makes sense in it own local 3-D context, but as a whole, the triangle fails to make sense as a 3-D frame.

As noted above, in addition to the absence of independent objects (corners), the context is never observed. It is not an arising in direct experience. Rather, it is an idea that is extracted from the objects and their relationships; a bit like the urge to find a pattern within the dots on a page. Context makes sense of objects and their relationships, and related objects give rise to context. Independent confirmation of either objects or context is not possible, even in principle.[55]

The Penrose Triangle seems to me a good metaphor for how the objectivist view of reality lacks coherence. In our day-to-day lives we seem to get along with conventional objects because we take the context of objectivity as a given and skip nimbly from one object to another, assuming that what we see is real and assuming that we can know several real things at any one time. We can't, and we don't. Whatever experience is, it is whole, which is to say, coherent.

Deposits

I found the direct path in midlife, having modestly and quietly followed various flocks of wild geese over landscapes of environmentalism, various forms of Christianity, self-help, TM, New Age, Yoga, and Buddhism. And it took me a surprisingly long

55. Berkeley in his Essay "De Motu" followed similar reasoning in taking Newton to task over the latter's idea of absolute space, which was a necessary requirement for his mechanics. Berkeley held that absolute space is an abstract concept with no physical reality. In the terms developed here absolute space = pure context without objects.

time with the direct path to realize that I had pitched-up with a very strong realist outlook and that I continued to cherish the notion of finding out for sure The Way Things Really Are.

Medical science is deeply invested in the reality of the body and its mechanisms; for the science of psychology the same might be said of mind. Geology is a deeply synthesizing science seeking to establish coherency within, and relationships between, complex three-dimensional expressions of soils and rock strata within a highly conceptualized understanding of time. As a geologist, the concrete reality of the spatial and temporal distributions of matter was deeply ingrained, objectively real and packed a huge punch of reality effect.

My wrestling with the idea of objects at a distance as described above reveals an ingrained and habitual desire to find the answer: separation seems to be real—but how?

The notions of triangulation, reality effect, and gestalt prompted by Berkeley and developed in the direct path were key ideas among a few others that, in retrospect, I needed to explore in order to reveal the tangled birds nest of assumptions of my worldview. Gradually these ideas led me to those places where I began to hear the message of non-separation contained in the direct-pointing teachings—teachings that work instantaneously for some people.

The chalk cliffs of southern England are gradually and evenly collapsing. The entire coast recedes in a more or less straight line, each collapse revealing fresh rock, while continual undercutting by the sea produces multiple small cliff falls. Occasionally large and dramatic cliff failures occur, but few people ever witness the drama. My enquiry with the direct path has mimicked this process, appearing as a series of insights or aha! moments. Each seemed like a breakthrough, but in time was released completely, in much the same way as a pile of collapsed chalk on the foreshore is quickly and totally dispersed by the sea in its gradual advance landwards.

In coming to better understand the flimsiness of objects and relationships and the convenience of objectivity, and knowing the saturating wholeness of experience, I realized that much of my enquiry had been probing the ontology of illusion. It wasn't a waste of time and effort—I needed to do it this way. It showed that my explanation of the illusion of objectivity, which was the fruit of fairly intense enquiry, was itself an object, with the same status as all the rest.

Whether understood as the products of perceptual triangulation or whatever, objects can still have meaning as things of beauty and utility and lots more besides, but we don't have to believe that they are fundamentally existent as separate entities. And if they aren't fundamentally separate or even extant... then are we?

What this enquiry revealed was there is no answer to the question, "What is the way things really are?" Objects, in the broadest sense, are not what we thought them to be, and the "way that they really are" is just another object.

At the foot of the Seven Sisters I sensed a kind of joyful awe of being merged whole with the environment; amongst the myriad of connections and ramifications, objectivity had loosened its grip. I have never felt the need to explain this. There is rarely a need to explain joy and happiness.

William Blake was right: as a man is, so he sees. But this insight and his communication of it conveyed more than mere accuracy; it spoke of connection and kindness.

Acknowledgements

My great thanks go to Greg Goode for his generous and enthusiastic elucidation of the direct path and for taking care and pains with my many questions over the years. Similarly, a big thank-you to Rupert Spira, who answered skilfully and wisely responded to great strings of questions from me at meetings.

Friends and members of the Direct Path Facebook Group have been and continue to be much appreciated. I'd like to gratefully acknowledge my friend Mandi Solk, who was the first to suggest to me that thinking has a felt component in the body, and deep thanks go to Rob Matthews, who introduced me to the idea of the felt sense in the body and helped me to develop the sensitivity to better come to know it.

> If we declare that there's only One
> Three at least must be
> Therefore it is said
> Not Two

Epilogue

Over a year since writing this essay, have I had any new insights and has my perspective changed? What has struck home and what have I internalised?

I seem to experience a settling in, a grounding, and an open-heartedness. I do still find myself looking for explanations, but it's more of a habit than a purposeful search.

Along the way I have learned about my own voices and the ways in which I think—it has been a fascinating trip. All that I am in objective terms, is characterised in relation to other things: and all things are defined in relation to "me", but objectivity itself is not what it seems.

The most profound and lasting (so far) effect is that I seem to have internalised this: ANY and ALL objects we think we know as separate things, including the reflex to search for explanations, exist without foundation. They are effectively called into existence: called and caller co-create. What is seen and what is heard depends on the voices of the caller; and the caller's vocal chords are fashioned by experience.

This co-dependency has similarities with emptiness teachings or what has also been called "non-reductive nonduality". Several years ago, on the advice of both Greg Goode and Rupert Spira, I steered my enquiries more towards the Direct Path and away from the Emptiness teachings. However, the gentle dissolution of objectivity has revealed in some strange way (to me at least), a kind of rapport between these two approaches. If I was to attempt a summary characterisation of their friendship:

Awareness teaches no relationships (because there are no real objects)

Emptiness teaches only relationships (because there are no real objects)

I am still interested in the ideas of triangles, relationships, trinities and triangulation despite, or even because of, the flaws noted in the essay. I also still notice the reflex to seek explanations, but it doesn't seem to be so very critical and urgent. I'm happy enough as an impossible triangle!

"If triangles made a God, they would give him three sides." [56]

---

56. "*Si les triangles faisaient un dieu, ils lui donneraient trois côtés.*" Charles de Montesquieu (1721) Lettres Persanes (Persian Letters) Lettre LIX

Any Day Now I Shall Be Released:
On Not Being "Finished" on the Direct Path
by Stephen Joseph

❝Using direct-path inquiry to examine the feeling of inadequacy, we can see that it […] is engendered by a sense of lack, but in this case the lack is in terms of objective standards that aren't being met. It derives its power from a belief in a sort of golden yardstick against which I can be measured. I can find all sorts of ordinary yardsticks to measure this body and mind against within awareness, but they are all conditioned and dependent. When it comes to applying a standard to my existence, especially when I take my stand as awareness, no such measure can be found. I have reaped emotional benefits from this realization, as measures against which I have fallen short my entire life have been seen through and dissolved.❞

Finding the finish-line

I'm not finished on the direct path. I have not become enlightened, pierced the veil, self-realized, dropped false identification, or achieved *moksha*, nirvana, or paradise. I have had glimpses, of various durations, that have revealed what I'm looking for, but they have stayed glimpses. It's as if I were flying to London and watching a travelogue about London on the plane, so I know it exists. I can even see it from my window. But the plane doesn't land.

This has been frustrating, but for me, the direct path continues to be inviting and seductive. Years of reading, inquiring, and conversing have not led to a complete breakthrough, but they have given me the faith that the remedy to the obstructions I encounter could well lie in the direct-path teachings themselves. My aim is that those who feel a similar frustration will find in this essay a companion in using the direct path to address those feelings thoroughly and honestly, and to discover what they might mean and also the blocks that might be giving rise to them.

What does being finished mean?

Every spiritual path, including nondual ones, generates an idea of being "finished" from its own perspective. Naturally there will be disagreements between paths about what being finished means. Followers within a path also disagree about what happens (or doesn't happen) after the path is completed. Is life problem-free? Are you the master of any situation? Can you enlighten others with a touch? Can you see through solid walls?

Just as a starving diner is more interested in the main course than in dessert, I'm not concerned here with the question of life after finishing. My definition of finishing the direct path is a permanent shift in perspective so that the world is no longer seen as a collection of separate physical objects existing apart from awareness, and exclusive identification with one's body and mind comes to an end. The best analogy I've heard to illustrate the permanence of this shift is that of a child who discovers that there is no Santa Claus. Contrary to popular Christmas movies, adults don't go back to believing in a literal Santa Claus.

I've been following direct-path teachings for about 10 years. I've read, met with teachers, watched videos, and done a great deal of intense questioning and pondering. I have been interested in spirituality since I was in my teens. Early flirtations with Judaism, the Baha'i Faith, and Zen gave way to other paths and teachers, most notably Douglas Harding[57] and J. Krishnamurti. What I was hoping for as an end-point for those paths was not very clear to me at the time.

Looking back, I think it was equal parts wanting to see how

57. Harding, D.E. (2013) *On Having No Head*, Sholland Trust.

things *really* are (if the way a bee sees an orange and the way I see it are different, which one is real?) and wanting to be seen as a sage, a teacher, one who knows. I care much less now about how I'm seen by others, possibly a side-effect of direct-path studies, possibly a side-effect of aging. I still enjoy sincere compliments (I didn't run them through that sincerity filter as I do now, but just took all I could get), but being on the receiving end of slights and indifference fails to affect me as it once did (but enough about family reunions!).

Periods of clarity

What I'll call periods of clarity have helped to keep me going on this path. They are the convivial inns along the way. When the clarity can be measured in just moments I can feel mental activity shutting down as I stare at the beauty of a random pile of litter, its simple is-ness revealed and shining, moving me emotionally for no describable reason. During minutes of clarity I've had a difficult discussion with a coworker become peaceful as resistance to him evaporates and non-defensive responses just emerge from me. When the clarity is measured in hours, a trip from the U.S. to Italy becomes almost stress-free. Airports, people, airplane interiors, more people, more airports successively pass through me while I, as awareness, remain absolutely immobile, never budging an inch. The usual worries and concerns of overseas travel arise and depart, never gaining a foothold. I suspect that being finished will mean no longer being able to measure this clarity with a watch or calendar.

Roadblocks

And I still have the motive of wanting to see how things really are. I wish I could say that the direct-path approach has sunk in enough that I know this is an impossible desire. I can repeat that there is no God's-eye view, no place to stand without a specific perspective in order to get a look at an external reality, and no external reality in any case. But I know that the idea of an external reality still has a hold on me. I've come close enough to dismissing it to feel a vertiginous thrill, a scary freedom, but, in the end, my solid feet come to rest on a solid floor, which rests on a solid earth, and then it's turtles all the way down.

With the help of teachers and writings, I've examined what seem to be the blocks that are standing between me and finishing. I have picked up some pointers that I think are promising, and that I'm still working on. Most of what follows is what I use to keep myself inquiring. For this essay I will focus on some particular blocks that are generally right at hand—distracting feelings.

Feelings

Realizing that I still haven't rid myself of this belief in an objective physical reality brings about a constellation of turbulent emotions: frustration, fear, inadequacy, and doubt. These have become my four beloved companions on the path (they must be beloved because I've kept them around so long). I will examine these feelings here for two reasons: to uncover the false assumptions they hide about what being finished with the direct path means; and to show how a direct-path investigation of these feelings can dissolve their power over us.

Frustration

Even if this spiritual path de-emphasizes goal-directed behavior, it is difficult to not let a sense of pursuit of a goal sneak in. I do want my experience to be other than it is; I want my feelings of separation to be gone. I fuel this frustration by reading about figures I view as having achieved enlightenment, and then adding imaginative leaps to those stories. I create entire scenar-ios starring The Enlightened and then escape into them when I have problems at work or upon looking for the third time at a credit-card bill. In my mental theater, when you open the pack-age of goodies awaiting you on the other side of the direct-path finish-line, "frustration" is noticeably absent!

Most people experience the feeling of not having the life they want materially or emotionally; I add "spiritually" to that roster of frustration. But looking closely at this frustration uncovers the hidden assumption that the direct-path teachings take you somewhere that you currently aren't. "Path" is a famil-iar and useful metaphor, but the teachings serve more to render translucent the concepts that are obstructing your existing view than to move you to a better vantage-point.

The application of direct-path teachings to the feeling itself is fruitful. This feeling of frustration points to lack. I don't have something I want, or I'm not something I want to be. This kind of existential lack is different from the lack of something material, such as money. Material needs can be dealt with on the material level. But this deeper sense of lack cuts more to the bone. So, let us investigate: can this deeper, existential lack be found?

One basic pattern in direct-path inquiry is to try to find something, anything, that is separate from awareness. In trying to do this, my failure rate so far is 100%. When this sinks in, it leads to an appreciation or apprehending of awareness as always complete and whole, and the conviction that there is nothing off-stage waiting in the wings to enter and add something to the show. Any place a lack could be found vanishes.

Fear

Fear as well stems from unexamined assumptions about what the direct path views as "being finished." I was once at a non-dual retreat, and during a question session a participant about

15 years my senior posed a poignant question to the teacher. Very directly and with clear emotion he described his efforts on this path. He then referred to his age and asked, in about so many words, if he would be enlightened before he died.

I was so caught up in his sincerity that I don't remember what the teacher said. (Maybe if I listened better at these things I wouldn't need to be writing this essay!) I'm now closer to that questioner's time of life, and I have some similar concerns. Will I die before I "finish"? Will I have squandered a human life? These questions view being finished as an accomplishment and also as a possession. The direct path doesn't treat it as either, as it requires a separate self both to do something and to own something. This can't be found.

The direct-path teachings can be applied specifically to this feeling also. Fear points to the future: something that I don't want will happen or something that I want will not happen. The investigation of the past and memory can be duplicated here with the future and anticipation. But the future is never experienced directly. Thoughts and images of it are experienced as just that—thoughts and images. They never point to an actual future, but arise only in present awareness.

I resonate with the deep-sleep teachings of the direct path, although I know not everyone does. These involve inquiry into the continuity of awareness when the body and mind are in the dreamless deep sleep state. One major component is pondering the implications of awareness not being continuously present during this time. One attraction for me is that they show that awareness is not dependent on specific, or any, arisings. They point to the continuity of awareness when we would normally think of it as absent. As my identity seeps into the awareness side of things, specific feared arisings lose their power to inflict harm or even destruction, and my morbid fascination with them decreases as well.

Inadequacy

I've had a lifelong distrust in my ability to "do" philosophy. Encountering philosophical arguments in texts or in person has left me unsure of my own ability to follow arguments or to counter arguments that I intuitively don't trust. I majored in religion in college and stayed far away from philosophy classes. I have an inherent distrust of being manipulated by philosophical questioning. I don't feel smart enough or skilled enough to detect flaws in reasoning or assumptions. My deep attraction to direct-path work is a little contrary to this aversion, as it can have the flavor of philosophical inquiry, but I'm not put off by that. This might be due to the nature of the teachers I've encountered and the fact that various modes can be used in direct-path work (see especially Greg Goode's *After Awareness*[58]).

Still, when surveying my progress on the path, I sometimes find myself feeling that I'm not smart enough to follow all of the steps that lead to the apprehension of all as awareness. Being finished would disperse these clouds of inferiority. I'd have the sort of certificate that the Wizard of Oz gave the Scarecrow to attest to my abilities. But this feeling of inadequacy is rooted in the assumption that the direct path is the only path or is somehow superior to all others, and that to "finish" requires the ability to adhere to it. These assumptions are not part of the direct-path teachings.

Using direct-path inquiry to examine the feeling of inadequacy, we can see that it, like frustration, is engendered by a sense of lack, but in this case the lack is in terms of objective standards that aren't being met. It derives its power from a belief in a sort of golden yardstick against which I can be measured. I can find all sorts of ordinary yardsticks to measure this body and mind against within awareness, but they are all conditioned

58. See Reading List p.160

and dependent. When it comes to applying a standard to my existence, especially when I take my stand as awareness, no such measure can be found. I have reaped emotional benefits from this realization, as measures against which I have fallen short my entire life have been seen through and dissolved.

Doubt

My participation in various paths has not been as extensive as that of many fellow seekers. I've read widely but have not followed or practiced many different teachings. Combining this realization with my feeling of not being finished leads to doubts about my current choice. I know that I have previously felt strongly that there were better and worse paths, in near absolute terms.

But direct-path teachings have sunk in enough that I no longer frame the issue that way. I do, however, harbor doubts about the combination of this path and me. Is my makeup better suited to a different approach? I don't so much doubt the efficacy of the path as I do its efficacy for me. If this is true, that I'm not suited to the direct path, then I'm walking on a treadmill while people around me are walking on firm ground and actually getting somewhere.

Another factor in this feeling of doubt could be that much of the success I've had in life has come in the academic world, which has often led me to feel that I've sufficiently understood something on the first or second reading. But such premature grokking doesn't work (at least for me) in direct-path writings, specifically with Greg Goode's exercises in *The Direct Path: A User Guide*. (These are not quite like Douglas Harding's experiments. Harding has said that you "get" the experiment right away, but it might take a while to work out the implications.) It takes time and pondering for the impact of direct-path exercises to sink in. My usual conviction that, if I can describe a line of reasoning, it means that I have understood it doesn't work in this realm. The direct path challenges basic beliefs that I've held for decades about the very world I live in, and patience is required. Perhaps my lack of background in meditation or other spiritual disciplines is hampering me. Assumptions about finishing on the direct path fuel this feeling of doubt as well. These assumptions connect enlightenment or liberation to a specific set of teachings, rather than to a match between student and teachings.

We can inquire directly into the feeling of doubt, just as with the other three feelings. The points regarding the feeling of inadequacy are helpful here too. Doubt comes from comparing paths, and also implies a standard. It suggests that there is a right path or method and that I might not have found it. Direct-path teachings can refute this notion also. The impulse to rate paths as better or worse, or closer to or farther from the truth, is strong. It comes to the fore when we have chosen a path, and feel the need to defend it against all other choices. We want to be on the best path and will cite lineages and longevity to bolster the claim. Or we might see a value in the lack of lineages and longevity and hold those against other paths. Just as with the feeling of inadequacy, making this judgment means being able to stand somewhere that is apart from the path and apart from reality and comparing the two. If such a place existed it would be so crowded you wouldn't be able to see anything from there anyway.

My own spiritual path has not been characterized by an excess of commitment. The direct path is the one I've spent most time on. That could be because its teachings and pointings are readily turned on itself. This is appealing on an emotional level to a non-joiner like me. I do have periods of doubt (maybe if I just spent more time gazing into the eyes of a photograph of Ramana...) but these alternative paths are not shut down or portrayed as fruitless. They can be used and inquired into and seen as fellow non-fixed points in a non-fixed universe.

Feelings as arisings

Resolving these feelings seems to be an important step in the path both in and of itself and also in clearing the way to deal with other possible blocks with clarity.[59]

The direct path offers other ways of dealing with feelings such as the ones I've discussed in this essay. Above I was investigating them as if the feelings actually pointed to something real. Feelings can also be dealt with more globally, depending on where you are in your direct-path inquiry. If what you once saw as physical objects are now seen as arisings in awareness and not evidence of an external reality, and if you see your body in this way also, you are ready to deal with subtler arisings such as thoughts and feelings more comprehensively, cutting the root. I'm talking to myself here, reminding myself of what I've read, but supported in some small part by glimpses of clarity that provide the breadcrumbs telling me this is a real path. Fuller explication of this is best left to other writers.

Investigating the idea of "finishing"

Once you've called into doubt the certainty that your body is a physical object, walking around on physical ground, occasionally bumping into physical walls and chairs, other big shifts loom. The idea of "finishing" itself can be inquired into with questions like these:

❖ What does "being finished" even mean in the direct path?

❖ What is the role in my inquiry with regard to people who are seen as "finished"?

---

59. A caveat here—If these feelings are impinging on your daily functioning, some sort of therapy is certainly appropriate and not at all at odds with the approach of the direct path.

❖ If people are not separate containers of experience, what sense does it make to inquire into how a teacher-figure experiences life?

There comes a point at which questions like these transition from being matters for idle speculation and word-shuffling to being stones in your chest that obstruct your breathing. When they edge toward the latter is when they should be dealt with.

You've read this far so I should probably tell you that you shouldn't have. Most traditions speak against spending too much time speculating about the end of the path. It is seen as a waste of energy that could be spent on treading the path itself. Also, if you're striving for a major shift in perspective, how well can you even envision that shift from the perspective you now have? I understand these cautions, but I give in to the urge to speculate anyway. After years and years of work on this path, I want to leave nothing out when it comes to inquiring. Maybe an inquiry into being finished is not fruitful, but a mixture of frustration and hope drives me there anyway. I go against my own advice about when to address questions and broaden my inquiry to try to uncover a hidden key. And I share it in the hope that the alchemy of writing will be transformative.

The glimpses, the thrill of questioning basic assumptions, and the fellowship of genial companions and guides have all kept me on this path, through the frustrations, doubts, and fears. And, in turn, the path has quelled some other frustrations, doubts, and fears that were present in my everyday life. The times that this inquiry has held sway haven't just been nice experiences, but also messages from another perspective. With continued inquiry and a love for awareness, all fixed points might drop away and all will taste of freedom.

About the Authors

DAVID BOULTER lives in Derby, England, where he is a maths teacher at a large Catholic secondary school. David bought his first PC computer at the turn of the millennium, and his interest in spirituality was ignited two days later when he asked Jeeves all about astral projection. A long-term meditator, David spent several years in the AMORC Rosicrucian Order before discovering the direct path in 2013.

As his neighbours can confirm, David enjoys playing guitar. He also amuses himself producing cartoons digitally. David is married to Jane and has a teenage son, Jack.

****

KAVITHA CHINNAIYAN is an integrative cardiologist, wife, and mother. Spurred by a sense of dissatisfaction and an epiphany that no material success could dissipate it, she began the inward journey. She has studied Advaita Vedanta, yoga philosophy, and Kashmir Shaivism with various teachers. In 2013, she was led to the direct-path teachings of Greg Goode and Sri Atmananda Krishna Menon. She lives with her husband, two daughters, and beloved dog in Michigan, where she practises cardiology, teaches meditation, and holds regular classes, workshops, and retreats on yoga, tantra, and nonduality. She enjoys writing, travelling, reading, and spending time with her family. Since contributing to this anthology Kavitha has published two books.

****

After 45 years working as a software developer, software architect, and CIO, STEVE DIAMOND recently began a second career teaching mindfulness. His interest in spiritual pursuits dates to his teenage years. Alan Watts and Robert de Ropp were early influences. From 1975 to 1998 Steve studied nondual philosophy with Kenneth Mills. More recently he's participated in many internet groups about nonduality. He has followed the direct path since 2013.

A lifelong lover of music, Steve holds a Bachelor of Music degree in theory and composition. He has sung in vocal ensembles including the Lane Justus Chorale and the Tucson Symphony Orchestra Chorus. Steve was born in New York City and now lives in Tucson, Arizona, where he enjoys music, art, hiking, reading, and writing.

****

PRISCILLA FRANCIS, the youngest of a large family, grew up in a diverse and accepting atmosphere. Though raised by devout Catholics, her formative years in Kuala Lumpur weren't dogmatic or regimented but included a variety of cultural, philosophical, and religious ingredients, wherein everyone was encouraged to be uniquely themselves.

Thanks to her early years in which spirituality was centred and embedded in daily living, she feels naturally inclined to deepen her insights by simply extending the explorations to fresh environs. She continues to intuit her own evolving pathways via a stimulating tapestry of experiences woven from threads of various spiritual foundations as well as those of her everyday life events.

****

JAMES NELSON HURLEY lives in midtown Manhattan with his wife Marcela Pulido, having arrived in Manhattan originally interested in pursuing a career in acting.

His creative interest turned within, due to an extraordinary experience he had on stage. In a scene studies class he had an epiphany: he transcended his persona and became the character. After he returned to his seat, he marvelled at what had just happened and wondered what that experience was. Where did it go? Why wasn't it here now?

Reading books by Abraham Maslow, Fritz Perls, Norman Vincent Peale, and ultimately meeting in 1976 his first teacher, Lester Levenson, he learned the Sedona Method Release Technique, which he taught for 20 years.

His initial pursuit still burning, James was led to Francis Lucille and the direct path in 1995. In 2003 James became certified in hypnosis and practised in Colombia and New York City until 2015. He now enjoys NYC theatre, photography, walks in Central Park, yoga, and travelling with his wife, always with Francis Lucille, Ramana, Nisargadatta or Atmananda close at hand.

****

STEPHEN JOSEPH is the Dean of Humanities and Social Sciences at a community college and teaches a course in world religions. He has been engaged with various spiritual teachings since his late teens, originally inspired by Alan Watts and J. Krishnamurti. He lives in Pittsburgh (USA) and enjoys spending time with his family, travelling, and nurturing delusions of adequacy.

****

In 2008, KIM LAI went to a Tony Parsons meeting, which sparked an interest in nonduality. He discovered the direct path at a meeting with Rupert Spira, which led him to the teachings of Jean Klein, Francis Lucille, Greg Goode, and Atmananda. Kim lives with his wife and three daughters in Sydney, Australia, where he runs the Sydney Non-Duality Meetup group. He likes literature, cinema, and comics.

****

JOHN LAMONT-BLACK trained as a geologist and undertook his doctoral research work on the chalk of southern England. He is presently the managing director (CEO) of a small geotechnical engineering company that he founded with academic colleagues from original research in university. John's inquiries have encompassed Christianity, New Age, TM, Zen Buddhism, and nonduality. While exploring broadly throughout his earlier years, at the age of 40 he encountered the teachings of the direct path through Rupert Spira and Greg Goode and has been carried along to this day. John lives with his wife in Edinburgh and enjoys long-distance mountain trekking, fell running, and hill-walking, especially in the Highlands of Scotland.

****

TERRY MOORE'S lifelong interest in mysticism took him down many roads before he finally came to a traditional perennialist universalist perspective and the practice of Sufism, which he has recently found to be greatly enriched by the direct path. He lives in New York City, and enjoys Islamic geometry as it reveals the underlying unity behind the veil, and studying Arabic. He is active with the TED organization.

****

SANDRA PIPPA lives with her husband in the village of Katonah, an hour's drive north of New York City. They are recently retired from the wine-importing business and spend time debating whether to move away. Sandra has been interested in paths of self-inquiry for many years. She enjoys gardening, cooking, reading, and walks in the woods.

****

ZACHARY RODECAP is a public-school teacher in Portland, Oregon, where he lives with his family. Prior to the direct path, he explored nonduality through Korean Zen, the Ordinary Mind School of Zen, and Toni Packer. He enjoys writing and commuting by bike.

Reading List

The following works are a selection of the nondual wisdom teachings inspired by Sri Atmananda (Krishna Menon). The list (alphabetical by author) is not exhaustive, but it does include the representative, well-known works in this field.

Sometimes this line of teachings is referred to as the "direct path," though that term is also used in a broader sense to include Ramana Maharshi, Nisargadatta Maharaj, and others. All these sources of wisdom agree that self-knowledge isn't achieved through a developmental process such as quieting the mind or becoming less attached to things. In this sense they are all "direct."

By (or featuring) Sri Atmananda (Krishna Menon)

Nitya Tripta (2009) *Notes on The Spiritual Discourses of Shri Atmananda (3 volumes)*. Non-Duality Press

Atmananda: Atma Darshan and *Atma Nirvriti*. [out of print]

By Greg Goode

Goode, G. (2009) *Standing as Awareness: The Direct Path,* (Revised Edition), Non-Duality Press

Goode, G. (2016) *The Direct Path: A User Guide,* Non-Duality Press

Goode, G. (2017) *After Awareness: The End of the Path,* Non-Duality Press

By Jean Klein

Klein, J. (2016) *Be Who You Are,* Non-Duality Press

Klein, J. (2016) *Who Am I?: The Sacred Quest,* Non-Duality Press

Klein, J. (Jan 2019) *Open To The Unknown*, New Sarum Press
Klein, J. (Jan 2019) *Transmission of the Flame*, New
 Sarum Press

By John Levy

Levy, J. (2004) *The Nature of Man According to the Vedanta*,
 Sentient Publications

By Francis Lucille

Lucille, F. (2008) *Eternity Now*, Non-Duality Press
Lucille, F. (2006) *The Perfume of Silence*,
 Truespeech Productions
Lucille, F. (2006) *Truth Love Beauty*, Truespeech Productions

By Philip Renard

Non-Dualisme (Non-Dualism, in Dutch)
*'I' is a Door: The essence of Advaita as taught by Ramana
 Maharshi, Atmananda & Nisargadatta Maharaj
 Non-Dualism: Eastern Enlightenment in the World of
 Western Enlightenment* https://tinyurl.com/ya3gqtmh
 (accessed 25 Aug, 2017)

By Rupert Spira

Spira, R. (2017) *Presence Volume I: The Art of Peace and
 Happiness* [2nd edition, revised]. Sahaj Publications
Spira, R. (2017) *Presence Volume II: The Intimacy of All
 Experience* [2nd edition, revised], Sahaj Publications
Spira, R. (2017) *The Transparency of Things: Contemplating the
 Nature of Experience* [2nd edition, revised], Sahaj
 Publications

By Ananda Wood

Some teachings from Shri Atmananda (Krishna Menon)
    https://tinyurl.com/yc39gabu (Accessed 26 Aug, 2017,
    at which time some of the internet links in this
    document were no longer active)
    https://tinyurl.com/y9hta29f [accessed 17 Oct 2018]
    https://tinyurl.com/y9lexjdf [accessed 17 Oct 2018]

Appendix: The Heart Opener

"The Heart Opener is a way to emphasize more directly the loving aspect of your nature as awareness. It is also an antidote to feelings of nihilism. It counteracts despair and hopelessness. If doing Self-inquiry hasn't provided a sense of sweetness, then The Heart Opener just might do the trick!"[60]

****

Before you begin[61]

Immediately before doing an experiment, take a few minutes to try what I call the "Heart Opener." It is akin to falling in love with awareness. It is akin to a reminder that awareness is the nature of you and all things. Experiencing this reminder opens the heart, and you'll find more ease and less resistance when doing the experiments themselves.

Being awareness – The Heart Opener

1. Take a deep breath slowly. Exhale slowly, all the way. Take another deep breath. Exhale all the way. Now take three-quarters of a deep breath and exhale as you normally would.

2. Close your eyes. Notice that there might be sounds, sensations, feelings and thoughts arising, but that YOU, the witnessing awareness to which these things are arising, are always already present.

---

60. From *After Awareness* pp.104-5. See Reading List p.160
61. From *The Direct Path: A User Guide*. See Reading List p.160

3. Notice that you are this clarity. You are present whether there are objects arising or not. **If there are objects**, you are already there as THAT which knows the **presence** of the objects. **If there are no objects**, you are already there as THAT which knows the absence of the objects. Regardless of the presence or absence of objects, you are there.

4. Notice that you are not an observed object at all, but the open, spacious, brilliant clarity in which objects arise. You cannot grasp or hold this clarity, for it is the very spaciousness in which grasping arises.

5. Notice that there are no walls to this clarity, no edges to YOU. You are borderless. You are not contained by anything. You are limitless.

This doesn't have to take long. You can do it just until you get a taste of yourself as this limitless awareness. There is a sweetness to this taste, which will cause you to fall in love with awareness all over again. And then when you do the experiments, it will guide you home.

****

"This opening of the heart can't be owned. You can't grasp and hold on to this clarity. You can't keep it around because something feels so good. The reason you can't grasp the clarity isn't a matter of the clarity being subtle and slipping out of your grip. Rather, it's because you already are this clarity. If a grasping desire happens, it isn't even 'yours.' It's just a temporary object arising against this same background of clarity that you are."[62]

---

62. From *After Awareness* pp.104-5. See Reading List p.160

Index

A

Advaita 46, 82
Anxiety 9, 31, 69
Atmananda. *See* Menon, Sri Atmananda Krishna
Autopilot 10, 40
Awakening. *See* Enlightenment
Awareness
  as always present 47, 81
  as a container 88, 94, 127
  discovery 2, 40, 81
  as endpoint of inquiry 103, 137
  of God 24
  standing as 10, 48, 82, 96
  and thought 104

B

Beliefs 106
Berkeley, George 127–130
Bible 57
Blake, William 125, 141
Body 83, 87
Buddha 78
Buddhism 119

C

Causality 66. *See also* Direct path, and causality
Color 49, 95, 102. *See also* Inquiry, color
Compassion 119
Consciousness
  as contained 87
  levels 39
  transitions 39, 39–40, 40
Curiosity 56, 63–64, 96–97

D

De Ropp, Robert S. 32, 39
Direct path
  benefits 2, 34, 37, 64, 67, 68
  and causality 60, 64, 67
  defined 19
  and doctrine 24
  and emptiness teachings 121
  goal 145, 153
  and language 90
  and nihilism 21
  obstacles
    doubt 151–152
    fear 148
    feelings 147, 153
    frustration 147–148
    inadequacy 150–152
  philosophical rigor 48–49
  and religion. *See* Religion and the direct path
  and religious experiences 26
  starting point 26, 37, 81, 99
  systematic approach 34
  teaching lineage viii
Distance 126, 130–132, 134

E

Effort 25
Ego 78
Emotions 72–73, 74. *See also* Inquiry, emotions
Emptiness teachings 118, 119, 122
Enlightenment ix, 30, 32, 42, 144
Escher, M. C. 138
Experience, direct 128

G

God 24, 57
Goode, Greg 89, 150

H

Harding, Douglas 145, 151
Hearing 35
Heart Opener 36, 121, 163
Heim, S. Mark 122

I

Ibn 'Arabi 26
Ideas 128
Inquiry
  beliefs 107
  color 49, 92, 102, 132
  counting 100–101
  distance 130–132
  emotions 61
  finishing the direct path 153–154
  hearing 35
  I-sense 81
  and love 10, 12
  mathematics 99–100
  motives for 89, 91
  and parenting 8–9
  perceptions 62–63, 80, 91, 103
  purpose 11
  seeing 92, 126, 131
  space 52, 89, 93, 126
  thoughts 104
Insecurity 73
Intuition 111, 123
Invocation of the Name of God 20, 23
I-sense 75, 76, 81. *See also* Self, separate
Islam 25

J

Joyful irony 12, 14

K

Kinaesation 133, 135

Kinaesthetic topography 133
Knowledge, conceptual vs. lived 19–20

L

Levenson, Lester 72, 73, 75
Lucille, Francis 77, 78, 81, 82

M

MacLaren, Leon 116
Master Game 32, 39
Memory 63, 65
Menon, Sri Atmananda Krishna 2, 79, 85, 89, 118
Middle Way 114–115
Mirroring 103
Mysticism. *See* Religious experiences
Mysticism and orthodoxy 17, 18

N

Nihilism 21
Nonduality
  defined vii

O

Objectivism
  and science 45
  and verification 51, 53
  as worldview 43, 51, 53, 115
Objectivity 93, 128, 129
Orthodoxy
  benefits 18
  defined 17
  and mysticism 17, 18

P

Parenting
  and authenticity 3
  and ego 4–5, 7
  and inquiry 2–3, 8

modeling behavior 5–6
  and rules 13
Penrose Triangle 138, 139
Perennialism 16

R

Reasoning, higher 2
Releaser. *See* I-sense; self, separate
Religion and the direct path
  harmony 26
  morality 22
  nihilism 21
  practice and environment 20
  realization of doctrine 20
Religious experiences
  defined 28, 29
  "pushers" 31–32
  states 33–34, 37, 38
  and tradition 25
Reutersvärd, Oscar 138
Roshi, Suzuki 43

S

Schuon, Frithjof 16, 17
Sedona Method 71, 72–75
Self, separate 45, 76, 79, 82, 115. *See also* I-sense
Sensation. *See* Inquiry, perceptions
Sexism 112, 116–117, 119, 120
Sleep 39
Smit, Paul 117
Soul 24, 25
Space
  experience of 87, 89
  inquiry 52, 136
  as location of mind 87
  nature of 86
Spira, Rupert 47
Sublation 88
Suffering 2, 59, 71, 72, 78, 89, 119

Sufism 22, 23, 24
Suspension of disbelief 106, 108

T

Time 135–136
Tolley, Dorine 116
Triangulation 134–135, 136–138
Trungpa, Chögyam 33
Truth 44, 104, 107

W

Watts, Alan 31
Women 112, 120

Y

Yoga 59

Z

Zen 45, 47, 52, 83

New Sarum Press

New Sarum Press published its first two titles in December 2018. The company is Julian and Catherine Noyce's second publishing venture; their first, Non-Duality Press, was bought in 2015 by New Harbinger Publications, San Francisco, where it continues to publish as a discrete imprint.

With the same degree of integrity, at New Sarum Press we are committed to offering books which address the ongoing dialogue between the traditions of Eastern wisdom and Western philosophy and psychology. Non-Duality Press was one of the earliest publishers to unpack and explore the contemporary expression of awakening and enlightenment. It also asked if these concepts are definable, valuable or even ultimately misleading.

New Sarum Press has a wider remit. We still publish the leading guides of the consciousness movement but we are open to books on the perennial philosophy, the counter-culture and its history and the healing arts and therapies. The question we ask of any submitted manuscript is, 'is this book accessible and relevant to our readers?' And, 'is this an original and positive contribution to personal growth and wellbeing as well as the wider healing of the planet?'

Unlike some larger publishers, we work as partners with our authors, we divide the income from book sales equally and offer them our many years of experience in the niche publishing industry.

CONVERSATIONS ON NON-DUALITY

Twenty-Six Awakenings

edited by Eleanora Gilbert

The book explores the nature of true happiness, awakening, enlightenment and the 'Self' to be realised. It features 26 expressions of liberation, each shaped by different life experiences and offering a unique perspective.

The collection explores the different ways 'liberation' happened and 'suffering' ended. Some started with therapy, self-help workshops or read books written by spiritual masters, while others travelled to exotic places and studied with gurus. Others leapt from the despair of addiction to drugs and alcohol to simply waking up unexpectedly to a new reality.

The 26 interviews included in the book are with: David Bingham, Daniel Brown, Sundance Burke, Katie Davis, Peter Fenner, Steve Ford, Jeff Foster, Suzanne Foxton, Gagaji, Richard Lang, Roger Linden, Wayne Liquorman, Francis Lucille, Mooji, Catherine Noyce, Jac O'Keeffe, Tony Parsons, Bernie Prior, Halina Pytlasinska, Genpo Roshi, Florian Schlosser, Mandi Solk, Rupert Spira, James Swartz, Richard Sylvester and Pamela Wilson.

CONSCIOUS.TV
Cherry Red Books

41100476R00115

Printed in Poland
by Amazon Fulfillment
Poland Sp. z o.o., Wrocław